EXPLORING ENGLISH WITH MICROCOMPUTERS

MEP Readers 1

EXPLORING ENGLISH WITH MICROCOMPUTERS

edited and introduced by
Daniel Chandler

Published in association with the
National Association for the Teaching of
English by the Council for Educational
Technology on behalf of the
Microelectronics Education Programme

In association with the National Association for the
Teaching of English, published and distributed by the Council for
Educational Technology, 3 Devonshire Street, London W1N 2BA,
on behalf of the Microelectronics Education Programme,
Newcastle upon Tyne Polytechnic,
Cheviot House,
Coach Lane Campus,
Newcastle upon Tyne NE7 7XA

First published 1983

ISSN 0264-4142
ISBN 0 86184-102-6

Chandler, Daniel
    Exploring English with Microcomputers — (Microelectronics
    Education Programme Readers, ISSN 0264-4142; 1)
    1. English language — Study and teaching
    2. Microcomputers
    I. Title   II. Series
    420'.7'10285404   PE1128

    ISBN 0-86184-102-6

Printed in Great Britain by
H Cave & Co Ltd
Cumberland Street
Leicester LE1 4QQ

Contents

Preface

Before you close this book, having glanced only at the first few pages, let me reassure you that it is not a book about programmed learning edited by a computer scientist. I have been an English teacher in comprehensive schools for seven years, and I reject computerized programmed instruction just as I would reject 'slot-and-filler' texts purporting to teach 'Spelling' or 'Grammar'.

I hope that this little volume will be of interest to English teachers who are intrigued, amused or even shocked by the idea that computers can have anything to do with a subject in which imagination and sensitivity play so great a part. It is not primarily a practical 'A to Z', but a series of perspectives on the field intended as a focus and stimulus for a discussion of issues and possibilities. Nevertheless, it does contain practical starting points for the teacher who is keen to experiment with this exciting new resource.

I dedicate it to Don — the most creative wordprocessor I know.

Words of thanks

I would like to express my hearty gratitude to all the contributors who cheerfully agreed to produce their papers within a period of only three weeks; but my warmest thanks must be reserved for Richard Fothergill and Bob Coates of MEP, who needed so little persuasion to agree to publish this book, and who were reckless enough to allow me to edit it.

My apologies to my wife Rose and my son Robin who have had to put up with my retreat to my study for most of the Christmas holidays.

Daniel Chandler
December 1982

National Association for the Teaching of English

In 1981, a local branch of the National Association for the Teaching of English organized an evening meeting for its members on 'Microtechnology and its implications for English teaching'. There were raised eyebrows, and one teacher expressed his puzzlement clearly: 'I didn't know there were any implications for English teachers'. 18 months later, a concerted demand came from heads of English departments, and from primary teachers, for a full conference to guide them in the way they spent money on — and used — the computers becoming available.

Computers are already present in schools, and indeed in English departments. This collection shows us pioneering work, and gives us signposts for the ways ahead. Above all, the book is a declaration that we should all look for ways of integrating what computers can do with the best kinds of English teaching.

I cannot speak for all members of the National Association for the Teaching of English, but as its present Publications Officer, I welcome this book and its programme for action which presents itself to all thinking teachers.

Mike Torbe, *Publications Officer*
National Association for the Teaching of English

Most of us are very ill-informed in this field and would like to become less so. While sharing both the usual unease of 'humanities' people confronted by rapidly growing technology and the fear that commercial exploitation may prove threatening to the role of language and literature in individual growth, we would recognize the special contribution teachers of English ought to make towards a discriminating understanding and use of new modes of communication. Our interests would extend from utilitarian matters of the so-called 'basics' (spelling, etc), through the processes of editing and rewriting, to the more sophisticated areas of semantics (language for definition, classification, and the like) and perhaps of more imaginative uses of language. Those of us with an interest in pedagogic linguistics might add a speculation on the relevance of computer-assisted learning to an understanding of language in gerneral and of the relationships between English and other languages.

Dr W H Mittins, Honorary Secretary
National Association for the Teaching of English

Introduction

Daniel Chandler, English Coordinator, Computers-in-the-Curriculum Project, Chelsea College, University of London

This is not the place for a full introduction to the theory of educational computing, but it may be useful to begin by explaining that most of the uses of the computer outlined in this volume represent an approach in which the computer does no more than act as a learning aid. It is an approach usually referred to as 'computer-assisted learning' or CAL, to distinguish it from the use of the computer for instruction ('computer-assisted instruction' or CAI), or for monitoring the learning process ('computer-managed learning' or CML). One of the contributors — Richard Knott — concludes his article by saying that 'it all depends upon which half of the equation you lay the stress — on teaching or learning. In my view', he continues, 'there should only be learners and facilitators of learning'. It is a view which I, and I believe many of the contributors, would share, and it is in this spirit that I shall examine the uses of the computer for mainstream English.

A writing instrument

Children are so used to being told to produce writing in schools that for most of them (and also for their parents) any other classroom activity, such as discussion, cannot be described as the 'work' with which they have come to associate school. And yet the amount of time spent on generating all this writing is far from justified by the worth accorded to it by anyone — including the writers themselves. Most of the writing consists of short bursts of spontaneous and often discontinuous text produced as quickly as possible to meet the demands of an audience of one — a teacher, whose response is frequently simply to skim-read it (often for errors) and to assign it a 'grade' according to its standard of factual and mechanical accuracy.

Most English teachers are acutely aware of these criticisms and have tried to encourage children to produce fewer pieces of writing, concentrating rather on gradually progressing from rough drafts to more satisfying and extended end-products which can sometimes be shared with a larger audience. But the difficulties here are enormous. Students are seldom keen to revise writing, and, even in classes where drafts are accorded real importance, redrafting tends to be confined to correcting spelling or punctuation rather than developing ideas and improving phrasing. And as for reading each other's writing: the idiosyncracies of immature handwriting can be so offputting even to the writer that the inevitable, if unconscious, comparisons with adult literary forms in print are seldom an encouragement.

The response of a keen teacher to this barrier to the sharing of writing may be to arrange for at least some of it to be typed out neatly and perhaps duplicated and circulated. Where this is done at all it is usually done by someone other than the writer. To see one's writing neatly typed out for you is of course a considerable (if infrequent) encouragement. Those lucky enough to have access to a typewriter for children to use themselves need not be reminded of how motivating even such a limited approach to print by the writer can be, however poorly it may compare to an experienced typist's efforts.

But the microcomputer when used as a wordprocessor might have been purpose-built to cope with these problems. As Anthony Adams writes in his paper, 'With the computer as a writing instrument . . . students . . . can gain the immediate and personal satisfaction of seeing their work as they would like it to be presented'.

Students can take advantage of the typewriter-style keyboard and instantly produce on the screen text which is always neat and attractive. Errors can be removed by the writer without trace as soon as they appear (and the consistent appearance of words on the screen makes the spotting of such slips so much easier). The text can be stored on ordinary audiocassette tape or on special 'floppy discs' for later use, making it possible for multiple copies to be printed out as and when required, with whatever modifications may be desired. A word, incorrectly spelt, may be replaced throughout the text when the student spots the error. Sentences and paragraphs may be shuffled around, inserted or deleted, allowing the writer to work through several versions (printing each out if necessary) without extensive and mind-wasting rewriting. Paul Moylan, a fourth-year student at Stantonbury Campus, discovered these advantages for himself 'All my life I have had trouble with my handwriting . . . This means that I always take a long time to write . . . The process that it takes to write an essay or story goes like this: first draft, usually a second draft and then writing it up into neat. This means that I take a long time writing and very little time being creative. With a wordprocessor I can write out my first copy . . . making any corrections that I want to make . . . (and then) . . . print it out.'

As with the typewriter, the microcomputer is (at the time of writing) too scarce a resource in schools for wordprocessing to be used with sufficient regularity for it to have any widespread dramatic impact on the problems outlined above. However, to ignore its increasing availability as a resource for children on a scale already far exceeding that of typewriters would be myopic. Within only a few years it may well be as reasonable to expect an English department to be engaged in the routine use of wordprocessors as it would be unreasonable now to expect most of them even to have seen one.

As Don Clark neatly observes in his article, 'Computers are particularly efficient at manipulating words and students have the potential to manipulate meanings. They really ought to get together during English lessons'.

Other contributors argue the case for the use of the computer not just as a writing instrument, but as a writer's aid, capable of performing far more sophisticated tasks than the latest typewriters with electronic memories. George Keith, whose pioneering work in developing the first A-level in English language will be well-known to English teachers, outlines in this volume a project on which he is engaged to develop software (computer programs) allowing children to use the computer as a wordhoard which will be far more flexible and useful than any adult thesaurus. By using the computer as a language tool rather than for programmed instruction, he suggests that we 'may actually rescue English language from ineffective mechanistic approaches'.

This is a theme pursued by Mike Sharples in his outline of his research. Regarding the computer as 'a construction kit for language' he shows how a child can be given 'the experience of a research worker'. English teachers who have lacked the confidence to adopt a linguistic approach will soon have a powerful incentive to become partners in learning with their students.

Mike Sharples has already developed programs which allow students to manipulate their texts according to in-built principles of transformational grammar, and he is engaged in making such software available on the more common microcomputers. As soon as material such as this becomes available we will have the tools, in Anthony Adams' words, 'to change dramatically the things that we as English teachers are concerned with'.

A framework for talk
To these unfamiliar with the effect of computers in the classroom it may seem perverse to suggest that the use of computers can promote constructive discussion rather than inhibit it. Many teachers will have nightmare visions of silent and solitary children staring mindlessly and hollow-eyed at 'educational' arcade games called, say, SPELL-INVADERS or CAPS-MAN. But research studies undertaken so far show that in practice the use of the micro as a

learning resource leads to an increase in useful talk and collaborative activities. Jan Stewart's contribution to this volume is a perceptive exploration of this theme. She observes that 'allowing children to chat informally about whatever interests them may have a place in school but will not necessarily promote the use of language as a tool for learning. It is in both creating opportunities for and adding purpose to informal group discussion that the microcomputer can play a part'.

Such opportunities for discussion are often the result of what seems to me the main advantage of the 'micro' in formal education—its use as a management aid. A program such as ANIMAL (described in Jon Coupland's article) is no more than the conventional 'Twenty Questions' game on a computer. But without the use of a computer it would be quite impossible to motivate students and to manage the game with small groups at the same time as observing and developing the language and reference skills involved. Using this game in a library, students don't need to be told to use reference books, or to have a discussion on issues as abstract as how to formulate useful questions. They are motivated to do so within the structure provided by the game (which in this case allows them to 'teach' the computer). And the talk of such students can show an excitement in learning so often crushed by institutional education.

Roger Lewis wrote in the Spring 1978 issue of NATE's journal, English in Education, 'In its ten years of existence, this Journal has published articles which stress that worthwhile talk and writing are more likely to result when the teacher is a friendly, observant participant working by the child's side, rather than acting as an interrogator or corrector. But this is not an easy role to adopt'. It seems to me that sensitive use of a computer for some kinds of small-group learning activity can allow the teacher to be a 'friendly, observant participant'—a partner in learning situations where there are no right answers, only possibilities to be explored. As I argued in an earlier paper, the use of computer-assisted simulations can make possible a genuine discussion of possibilities which may normally result in posturing rather than real thinking, in clichés rather than in exploratory language. Chris Harrison in his article deals with this use of the computer from the English-as-a-foreign-language perspective, but 'what if?' is a question which deserves far more attention in the mainstream English classroom.

I would not argue that computer-based simulations should take the place of more conventional simulations—indeed they may be simply management aids used only at limited points in appropriate simulations, perhaps for complex calculations, for a fair management of the rules, or for adding a new dimension such as a graphic presentation which can be manipulated in a variety of ways. I have seen examples where the assistance which the computer can offer in structuring such activities has provided a chance for teachers to engage in an activity for which they may normally have lacked the confidence, and thus help to ensure that students are not starved of opportunities for vital kinds of talk that are often ignored in the secondary curriculum.

With computer-managed simulations, not only is the teacher freed of the management of the group using it, but students may be freed of the teacher. The discussion which takes place is not structured by the teacher, and tends to begin with a great deal of useful talk to establish ground-rules within the group. Then there will be an interplay of predictive talk, and the necessarily tentative expositional talk which is so often discouraged by a teacher-dominated structure. Excellent examples of computer simulation software which enables this kind of talk-shop to happen are the archaeological programs SAQQARA and MARY ROSE published by Ginn, developed by Ian Whittington and Barry Holmes for use across the curriculum in primary schools.

It would be sad indeed if the children from our primary schools who are rapidly becoming used to using microcomputers as a flexible learning resource in this way find that in secondary schools computers are regarded largely as the preserve of mathematics and science departments, to be used only as super-calculators by a privileged few.

Literacy skills for a new medium
Few teachers would dispute the need for children to learn something about computers, but most English teachers at present, even if they could be persuaded to use computers as a resource, would not see themselves as having any role to play in teaching *about* computers (although a handful might be involved in humanities courses examining their social implications). There is a real danger therefore, that where opportunities exist for children to learn about computers, (often, ironically, in 'computer literacy' courses), no attention will be paid to developing an awareness of the computer as an emerging mass medium, requiring skills which are in some ways extensions to the traditional literacy skills of reading, writing and fact-finding.

As I have argued elsewhere, screen-reading, keyboard and retrieval skills are not the same as reading, writing and fact-finding with other media. And yet 'computer literacy' (or even worse, 'computer awareness') courses tend to concentrate on the technology rather than on the medium. Marshall McLuhan warned us of the dangers of this blindness many years before the emergence of microcomputers. He declared that 'electric information environments alter our feelings and sensibilities, especially when they are not attended to'. Children may quickly become fluent in using a keyboard and reacting to prompts from a screen with daunting speed without any help from adults, but to assume that they are 'aware' of the medium and have acquired, for instance, efficient reading and information retrieval skills through use alone would leave them vulnerable.

Computers are becoming far more part of the everyday lives of children (and adults) than their present distribution in schools might suggest, and however well-designed educational screen displays may be, children need to be able to cope with reading many kinds of screen displays for a variety of purposes. These screens differ from printed pages in that their contents may change as you watch (words may move from right to left or from the bottom to the top of the screen), and even if they stay still, the premium on space may mean that the language is compressed in meaning and syntax. It is not as easy to browse as it is with a book, so frames are more difficult to compare than pages.

It may not take us long to familiarize ourselves with such new reading conventions (if we have the opportunity), but English teachers ought to be involved in helping to develop efficient reading strategies using the medium. Anthony Adams in his paper refers to the way in which the revolution in information technology makes it even more urgent for English teachers to concern themselves with developing reading skills other than simple reading and recall.

In a society in which information is already the key resource, and microelectronic technology is the most powerful means of rapid and comprehensive access, we all need to be 'information-wise'. We need to know how to formulate our needs, what kinds of sources are most appropriate, how to isolate the information and how to evaluate, record and use it. Patrick Scott's article shows how one English teacher has begun to use the computer for information-handling, concentrating on developing the skills of interpreting information retrieved from the computer. His students will never make the mistake made by one adult recently when a computer was installed at the new NATE office. The speaker declared that the members' changes of address would no longer be a problem — the computer would always know. As Patrick Scott's students discovered, the computer can only contain information if someone puts it there. We also need to learn that the computer will only answer the questions you actually ask, and not the questions you

14

ought to have asked. And even when you receive the information, it must be remembered that it is only as good as the person who provided it: people still tend to assign to computers the unassailable authority once accorded to print.

The book is not going to disappear, and neither are traditional reference skills. But in a rapidly changing world, 'tapping it out' is likely to be a more common resort than 'looking it up' for some purposes, and we need to be able to cope with additional skills with a critical awareness of a new medium.

The shortage of software

It would be unfair to pretend that there is a wealth of good software already available for mainstream English. There is, as various contributors point out, a mass of appalling drill-and-practice material which passes under the name of 'English' in the catalogues of some commercial software publishers. There is also a small amount of good educational software, produced by some of the centres of excellence in this field, which is either intended for or has applications in language development. Some of these have been referred to in Jon Coupland's article in particular. Further material specifically for mainstream English is at present under development by these national projects (and by commercial publishers) and will be appearing in the near future.

There are several reasons for the shortage of suitable software. Firstly, commercial software publishers have little idea of what English is about. Secondly, too few English teachers are involved in local program development groups: many who are interested haven't yet realized that they *can* become involved in program design or have little idea how to begin. Thirdly, existing projects developing software for English are only too well aware of the dangers, and producing a good learning package (of which a computer program is only one item) with part-time teams can take from one to two years. My own feeling is that this picture may well change rapidly within only a year or two, as the available software reaches what Steve Kennewell of Birmingham Educational Computing Centre recently described to me as 'the "critical mass" . . . required to detonate an explosion of ideas'.

Some have cynically commented that the reason for the lack of software is that the computer is 'a solution in search of a problem'. Such a fear certainly haunts some English teachers when they initially embark on program development, but this glib dismissal is hardly an adequate description of the vital phase of discovering what computers can do, before you can decide the best way to use them to meet your needs.

Those who feel that the need to act is urgent have three options. The first is to make a judicious selection from what is available, even if it was not produced for English. This is how I began in 1980, experimenting with the use of 'Adventure' games in mixed-ability English classes. Although I had bought mine as a single-player home entertainment game, I soon found out that it could be an amazingly motivating focus for a variety of group language activities. Interested readers will find descriptions of these extraordinary games in the articles by Derrick Daines and Jon Coupland. An account of my own use of them appears in a paper I contributed to Anthony Adams' recent book, *New Directions in English Teaching* (Falmer Press). A second strategy is to choose software which may not be adequate in its existing form, but which, with the help of some enthusiastic amateurs, you may be able to adapt to meet your needs.

The third option is to become involved in the design of your own programs. Let us be clear that we don't need to rush out and learn programming in order to design a program. This has indeed been a tragedy in some cases where teachers who previously channelled their creative energies into creating exciting learning environments have suddenly become 'computaholics', even to the point of inflicting on their students mechanistic exercises which they would otherwise have condemned with vigour. Good programs are unlikely to be written by amateur programmers such as busy teachers. On the other hand, professional programmers need to be told exactly what to produce if they are to meet teachers' needs. So what is required is a team approach.

At the early stages a programmer is not needed. But those involved need to work towards drawing up a precise 'specification' of the program. Jan Bright's article outlines some factors you need to bear in mind. A good way in which to approach this problem is to think in terms of what you want to appear on the screen, and when. If you tackle small areas of your program idea at a time (Seymour Papert uses the engaging phrase 'mind-sized bites') you can piece together a jigsaw of 'screen-charts' rather like a 'storyboard' for a film. The resulting charts should be clear to both the ordinary classroom teachers — who can see if the program is likely to meet their needs — and the programmer — who can tell you if your computer can cope with what you are proposing.

When you reach the stage where a programmer is needed there are several ways in which such support may be found.

1. Your school may have a computer studies department whose staff or students may be willing and able to produce at least a

prototype of your program idea. But don't depend on this because such kind volunteers may not be too happy if you want several revisions of the program, as you almost always will.

2. Your local MEP (Microelectronics Education Programme) regional information centre may be sufficiently interested in your idea to try to arrange for it to be programmed for you. Contact MEP headquarters for your nearest centre (see the address list at the back of this book).

3. Your local education authority may have a computing adviser who may put you in touch with an LEA programmer (if there is one).

4. If your idea seems a really exciting one you could approach one of the national projects to see if they might like to take it up (the addresses of ITMA, Chelsea College and AUCBE are at the back of this book).

This short book can do no more than sample the range of existing investigations into some of the possibilities of the microcomputer which have relevance for the English teacher. Lack of space has made a comprehensive review of the field quite impossible. No mention has been made, for instance, of the exciting work being done by Michael Clark in Newcastle using hand-held wordprocessors (called 'Microwriters'), of Derek Eccles, English adviser for Surrey, who has championed the case for using microcomputers with his fellow advisers, or of the many local groups of English teachers who have begun to devote a great deal of their own time to program development.

Indeed, such is the scale, recency and acceleration of these activities that this book (taken by the publishers with extraordinary rapidity from manuscript to print) will without doubt appear sadly dated as a survey within only months of its publication. I hope that the reader will find the revolution in attitudes of which this is a consequence as exciting an environment in which to work as I do.

Why English teachers should use computers

Anthony Adams, University of Cambridge Department of Education

Quite apart from the work of the Microelectronics Education Programme and the Department of Industry the speed with which microcomputers are being introduced into schools is remarkable enough. It is the one clear growth area in the provision of educational resources at the present time. Alongside this we must place the rapid growth of the use of computers in everyday life. A few years ago my high-street travel agents did not have so much as an electronic calculator; now every counter space has its own programmable computer and the evidence of instant communication throughout the world through devices as ancient as telex to those as modern as satellite communication is apparent. W H Smith and Boots now carry a wide range of home computers and associated software materials and the home computer is one of the most popular 'family' presents at Christmas time.

English teachers who, like myself, grew up in the world before all this started about ten years ago may well wonder what it has to do with them; especially as, at first sight, computers seem to be dauntingly mathematical. My argument would be that the widespread introduction of the microprocessors into schools and society is so important that we cannot afford to leave them to the mathematicians and scientists alone. What, above all, we need to avoid is a computer-educated élite which understands the implications of how computers work whilst the remainder of us are at the mercy of these mysterious machines and of the élite who program them. What I am really arguing for is a comprehensive programme of computer education in schools, a kind of computers-across-the-curriculum approach, which will ensure that all school-leavers at 16 have some understanding of this powerful tool which will affect their lives immediately and will continue to do so in the future in ways that are virtually unimaginable at the present time. For my money, the role of the teacher of English and the humanities needs to be central in this development and the target area in schools should be the 9 – 13 age range. To leave it to the upper forms of secondary schools and to deal with only the most able children in the science classes will bring about the worst possible social consequences of the computer revolution. It was a long time between the invention of printing and the development of the notion of universal literacy; in the case of computers we need to move much more quickly.

Yet, with all the talk currently going on and the millions of articles published in professional and popular journals on computers and education, the stress seems to be disproportionately upon the 'hardware', the computers themselves, and all too little upon *education,* the learning process, and the contribution that computers can make here. A survey of available computer software for educational purposes, especially in English, is disappointingly predictable — there are innumerable multiple-choice programs designed to 'help' children learn to read, pick out opposites to given words, memorize the authors of 'great books', learn the parts of speech. What we are seeing is the worst of the textbooks and workbooks of the past 30 years being served up in new guise as computer programs, with all the extra glossiness and stimulus provided by the introduction of clever graphics that will 'reward' a student for a 'right' answer. It is the final outcome of Skinnerian behaviourism misapplied in education and, because the computer terminal is very motivating and the students will work happily for hours inputting their answers to these meaningless tasks (after all, we know that they like doing workbook exercises and gap-filling already if they are not given something more worthwhile to do), parents (and some teachers) will really believe that some educational activity is going on and the high-street computer shops will make a good deal of money. It has been said that the microcomputer is 'a solution looking for a problem to solve'; even more significantly the man who has probably done most thinking about the applications of computers to education, Seymour Papert, has remarked: 'How strange it is that computers in education should so often reduce to using bright new gadgets to teach the same old stuff in thinly disguised versions of the same old way'.

In this short article I want to suggest that the widespread introduction of microcomputers into schools ought to change dramatically the things that we as English teachers are concerned with though, alongside this, of course, there will be many of the same old things (not, I hope, 'stuff') which we shall continue to teach with relatively little help from the 'bright new gadgets'. I don't see the microcomputer, in the immediate future, doing much to help me with the teaching of Jane Austen or Wordsworth, for example. But the teaching of writing seems to me a very different matter. At the very lowest (and most traditional) level I have seen computer programs that can effectively 'prompt' a student engaged in writing a story, urging, through a use of a series of open-ended questions, more specific detail about the weather, what a character looked like, was wearing and so on. Just as the old fashioned kaleidoscope could provide ideas for the artist to work on by suggesting possibilities, so such a computer program can help to get ideas flowing for the student who 'doesn't know what to write about' or who has problems over writing anything copiously.

But, of course, we can go much further than this when we begin to turn our microcomputer into a wordprocessor. At the very least, the ability to correct the first draft of a text with ease and with the avoidance of the tediousness of writing it all out again leads to a greater willingness on the part of the student to redraft and proof-read the work. The motivation of seeing it beautifully presented on screen or printed out is a very powerful one and provides a genuine incentive to 'get it right' in the student's own terms — just as my possession of an electric typewriter with an automatic correction facility has totally transformed the writing of this article from the labour it would have been a few years ago. Most of us have spent many hours typing out students' work for display and other purposes believing that one way to motivate and encourage the reluctant writers was to let them see what their work could look like, properly presented. Now, with the computer as a writing instrument, we can hand over that task to the students themselves and they can gain the immediate and personal satisfaction of seeing their work as they would like it to be presented. Both Seymour Papert and Frank Smith in recent books have commented upon the speedy and significant gains in written work that result when students are given access to a microcomputer to help them process their work.

Important though this is it is of far less significance than the more advanced aspects of the computer-as-wordprocessor when we begin to exploit its remarkable capacity, not just to help us in proof-correcting, but to enable us to manipulate text. Now, for the first time without laborious repetition, we can try out what we are trying to say in different ways, move paragraphs around, change and insert sentences, replace and substitute words and ideas, and still have a perfect copy for our final version. We can be encouraged, as few writers have ever been before, to experiment with a whole range of ways of saying the same thing and this can be done with no more tedium or physical labour than writing a first draft with pen or typewriter today. Joyce was reputed to have spent a whole day composing a 15-word sentence in *Ulysses,* trying out every possible combination of the words to give the meaning he was looking for. Now the wordprocessor brings the capacity to do this kind of playing around with what we are writing *while we are writing it* within the potential of every student in every classroom. (Wordprocessing at this level is not expensive; quite acceptable programs can be obtained to run on a machine as inexpensive as the Sinclair ZX81.)

My own guess is that the microprocessor has brought about conditions that will significantly affect our whole approach to the composing process and that, for the students and writers of the future, writing and composing will become a much less linear procedure than it has tended to be hitherto.

Of course, all this implies that the student has the appropriate psychomotor skills that enable screen-reading and the use of the typewriter keyboard to become second-nature. That phrase is used deliberately: we, teachers, often forget how unnatural the business of writing actually is, how difficult many of our students find it to manipulate their pens and to form their letters. It is a skill that has to be learned. Now, it can be very cogently argued, the new literacy skills that accompany the microcomputer age are the ones that should be being learned at the same time (that is in the infant school) and it should become the norm that by the age of six or seven most children will have as much familiarity with screen and keyboard as they have today with pencil and paper.

The second area on which I want to comment briefly is the use of the microcomputer as a means of accessing and ordering information. Among likely technical developments in the very near future will be the increased miniaturization of the computer itself so that we will be able to carry around with us a computer little bigger than present-day pocket calculators together with a flat, probably folding, plastic screen for viewing. (Indeed such developments are already with us and it is only a matter of time before the cost of using them falls dramatically.) Again, using technology already available to us, we can envisage a time—only a few years away—when by plugging into any convenient electric power supply and with the use of any telephone we shall have instant access to any databank stored on any mainframe computer anywhere in the world. In itself this will dramatically change the nature of what still passes for education in many of our schools. There will be no point in asking students to recall information as such; all the information in the world will be potentially theirs at the touch of a button. But this raises enormous problems of its own of course: the problem, above all, of being deluged by this information-explosion which is already taking place around us. We are getting increasingly conscious of the need to teach study skills but we ought to be thinking more of teaching information skills as such: how to ask the right questions, how to evaluate the answers and assess the value of one piece of information against another, how to sort out the relevant from the irrelevant, and how to process the information when we have received it. The secondary report of the Assessment of Performance Unit has shown us how limited most older secondary-school students are in their ability to work with text in this way as opposed to simple reading and recall. If we are not to leave them at the mercy of an information-saturated environment we shall have to do some hard thinking in the very near future about the implications of all this for the teaching of reading at all levels, thinking which has already been pioneered in the recent work done on the psycholinguistics of reading and the current work of Eric Lunzer and Keith Gardner at the University of Nottingham on 'Directed activities related to text.'

In this article I have deliberately concentrated so far on ways in which the microcomputer in the classroom will affect very traditional areas of the English curriculum in terms of reading and writing. But if we begin to get groups of students working at a single terminal—and for class management reasons this seems both desirable and likely—the use of the microcomputer as a stimulus to talking and listening becomes important too. (It also moves us away from the use of the computer with an individual student as a kind of enhanced language laboratory and so further away from pre-packaged behaviourist programs.) Daniel Chandler has written elsewhere of the use of commercially produced home-entertainment 'Adventure' games to act as a stimulus of this kind, and we are likely to see much wider and more intelligent, more open-ended, developments of this kind of material in the near future. Since in our society the ability to discuss, to negotiate, to come to consensus conclusions within the group becomes of ever-increasing importance it seems to me that the potential, as yet largely untapped, of this kind of approach to the use of talk in the classroom is of immense significance.

It was considerations such as the above that moved me and a group of colleagues in Bryanston Audiovision Ltd to call together a seminar in Cambridge in October 1981 to get educationists, teachers, publishers and manufacturers discussing how we might best work together to harness the potential of the microcomputer in the teaching of English and the humanities. Patrick Scott, who attended the seminar and wrote up a report on its findings, produced a diagram that summarizes in quasi-algorithmic form the way in which the new technology might affect humanities teaching. In a short paper such as this there has only been time to touch on those aspects that seem of most immediate (in 1982) significance to the teacher of English; by the time these words are read in published form in 1983 other things may well have moved into the forefront of our thinking. But all those areas identified in the diagram overleaf seem to me ones that teachers of English cannot afford to ignore. If we do so we shall be failing to prepare our students for the world in which they are going to live their adult lives and English

23

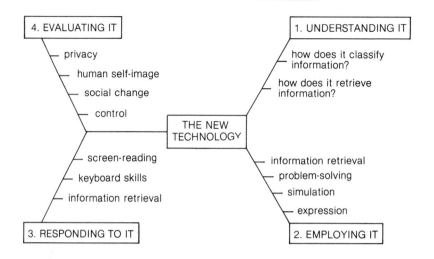

4. EVALUATING IT	1. UNDERSTANDING IT
— privacy	— how does it classify information?
— human self-image	— how does it retrieve information?
— social change	
— control	
	THE NEW TECHNOLOGY
— screen-reading	— information retrieval
— keyboard skills	— problem-solving
— information retrieval	— simulation
	— expression
3. RESPONDING TO IT	2. EMPLOYING IT

teaching will be in danger of becoming a quaint survival for the few in the way that the study of classics has become today.

In her very important book *Culture and Commitment* (1970), Margaret Mead makes a useful distinction between what she calls post-figurative and pre-figurative cultures:

'We must...teach ourselves how to alter adult behaviour so that we can give up post-figurative upbringing...and discover pre-figurative ways of teaching and learning that will keep the future open. We must create new models for adults who can teach their children not what to learn, but how to learn and not what they should be committed to but the value of commitment.

Post-figurative cultures, which focused on the elders—those who had learned the most and were able to do the most with what they had learned—were essentially closed systems that continually replicated the past. We must now move towards the creation of open systems that focus on the future—and so on children, those whose capacities are least known and whose choices must be left open.'

Because so much of the best English teaching since the war has moved in the direction of child-centred, open concept classrooms and away from simple notions of information-acquisition as education, the English teacher has a particular role to play in this development. Why should English teachers use computers? Because for their own sakes, the sakes of their students, and (possibly) the sake of the world itself they cannot afford not to do so.

Computer awareness and creative English – Mission Impossible?

Richard Knott, Adviser for English, Berkshire

Colour supplements advertise home computers with the kind of
aggressive confidence they once reserved for glossy sports cars.
'Educational programs', it seems, have all the answers: '...we have
a library of software to satisfy the most enquiring mind...' So we are
assured – and yet the advertisements show solitary children staring
into unexciting screens.

For years the assumption has been made by many of us that
computers are a mysterious adjunct to the teaching of mathematics.
In many local education authorities, maths advisers have been
burdened with the additional load of facilitating the expansion of
computer education into both primary and secondary schools. Just
over two years ago, as a head of English in a Bedfordshire
comprehensive school, I totally rejected the possibility that
computers might have any part to play in English classrooms:
'They're insensitive machines and they put people out of work', I
said, feeling secure in my liberal response. Some six months later,
at a conference of English advisers, the truth became clearer: that
computers are unavoidably about communication; that they can
store information and make it readily available for retrieval – both
powerful arguments for alerting teachers of English (and the
humanities) to their enormous potential as a resource. Yet not all the
advisers were convinced: having spent a taut afternoon
collaborating in groups in vain attempts to solve a computerized
simulation game – and arguably engaged in the most valuable kind
of 'classroom talk' – I heard someone say over dinner '... I can see
no place at all for the computer within the English programme'.

It's an attitude which is difficult to defeat: very recently one LEA
ran a course for English teachers entitled 'From talk to writing'
which included a workshop on computers as a small part of a much
broader package. Two teachers were almost prevented from
attending by a headteacher who asked 'What do you want to go for?
Computers are for maths.'

If the computer is regarded as no better than an electronic pest
by some, it can also suffer from bandwagon syndrome: a friend of
mine recently remarked of a trendy primary head: 'He's spending all
his money on computers – and yet there's no paper in the school'.
The machinery must be understood and used in conjunction with
other, more traditional ways of learning. Nothing could be more

likely to arouse suspicion than the use of the computer for either fatuous games or programmed learning.

In November 1981 the first workshop in the county on 'Microcomputers in the English classroom' was held at one of Reading's teachers' centres. The publicity for that first session emphasized the creative nature of the enterprise: 'The aim of this workshop is to investigate the exciting possibilities that the use of micros in English teaching opens up: in stimulating talk for example and in enabling students to learn to work together'. It quoted *The Times Educational Supplement* of a few weeks earlier: '. . . it would be a disaster if the introduction of micros led to long hours of children pointlessly practising basic English on a machine . . .' The workshop was essentially practical. Groups of teachers clustered around a clutch of machines loaned without charge by a Reading computer company (Berkshire has been unoriginally dubbed 'silicon Valley' and ICL analysts are thick on the ground!) For the most part teachers went away enthusing about the reality of their group's involvement and interaction, but we were all uncertain as to what might happen next. There were so many provisos, not least that the software available for English teachers seemed so poor. With no input from teachers versed in the best kinds of classroom practice, there was little active learning apparent and less imagination.

It was that realization that proved decisive: a working group of some dozen teachers, drawn from four secondary schools in the authority, was established. At the outset the group determined that its priority should be to produce its own software, aiming to explore the use of the computer as a resource in the areas of simulation games and information storage and retrieval. There was a strong determination to devise programs which were precisely tailored to the demands of good English teachers, rather than be constrained by the doubts of sceptical programmers. Two sub-groups were formed and the planning process began in earnest.

Both groups produced remarkably different 'programs', but with certain ground rules held in common. The computer, it was felt, should be just one more resource within the overall English programme: the activity or overlying project—'game' was dismissed as conveying too frivolous an idea of what was being devised! —should incorporate a whole range of typical classroom practice. Children would need to read associated printed sheets of information; they would role-play, talk and make appropriate decisions, write about the situation in a variety of registers and for different purposes. The class would be divided into groups of children all engaged in the same simulation, but working at different areas: they may be acquainting themselves with the introductory

26

'manual' that sets out the background to the situation, or selecting appropriate articles or stores to take with them on the journey being simulated (Mission Impossible!), or determining the roles they are to play... The important point is that the 'program' is but one part of a larger pack.

The need is for a context. A program, for example, which is specifically designed as a code-cracking exercise to be worked upon by a group cooperating and sharing ideas is likely to produce talk related only to the patterns of words and the frequency with which letters occur. Putting that code into an activity of which the code-cracking is only a part, but which the group *must* resolve in order to proceed, increases the motivation. Crucially too, the talk will become reflective—thinking back to previous events for clues—and predictive—tentatively exploring possible ways forward. There is something, quite simply, worth talking about.

It is right and proper that English teachers collaborate in this way: no concessions should be made, no shifting away from what we deem to be good practice. The scenario then could be something like this: small groups of children engaged in different tasks, but all related to the overall theme. In one corner, one group is tape-recording a report back to base; elsewhere another group is plotting a route across difficult country using a map; two children are deciding how best to explain the latest set of written instructions to the remainder of their group. The computer has a group of children beside it reacting to the consequences of earlier decisions displayed to them on the screen; another decision must be agreed by consensus and time is slipping away...

The Berkshire Micros and English group includes teachers from only four of the authority's 65 secondary schools and it is important that their work is disseminated and that help is given to interested teachers elsewhere who are daunted by what appears to be in-crowd jargon. 'Computer' is a word that doesn't exactly touch the soul: it smacks of statistics and conjures up threatening images of chattering printers spewing rows of incomprehensible figures. Software, memory, cassettes or discs... BBC Model B, 380Z, Sinclair... computer literacy, computer awareness, wordprocessors... The mystique must go and the machinery accorded as much, or as little, respect as a typewriter, taperecorder or television set. Typically, the children have adapted more quickly than we have: they are more at ease and accept the micro revolution without so much as a flicker of doubt.

The value of the computer as a further aid towards purposeful talk is considerable. It should not preclude, however, thinking about other possibilities and circumventing some potential hazards. It is not difficult to appreciate the potential of the computer as a wordprocessor in English classrooms. Many English teachers have come to recognize the need for children to redraft their writing, learning to shape both their experience and their attempts to set that experience down on paper. Writing is a craft that deserves time and thought. Unlike talk, you can choose at leisure when you wish to release your sustained expression to your audience. Looking back over the first draft of this—handwritten by Bic, no wordprocessor for me!—there are blue pools of correction scattered across the pages. The process isn't complete. The wordprocessor would make the redrafting far easier: the alterations, for example, can be typed in and the machine does the rest. Words can be deleted, syntax tampered with. As yet, however, we have done no real work to ascertain how best children can benefit: is it a resource to use, or a tool upon which to practise in isolation?

Computer literacy will become an area neglected by English teachers at their peril: if we don't make ourselves responsible, who will? But the skills of screen-reading, retrieving information and keyboard manipulation need to be incorporated into activities in which the imagination is stirred, the sense of motivation excited and the skills practised implicitly, rather than drilled. At least I think so! Future work for our teachers' group needs to focus on these areas of doubt and identify a policy upon which we can rely.

Attempting to develop interest and initiative in the field of micros and English has not been difficult up till now: willing, enthusiastic teachers from good departments have identified a need, developed a way of working and gone a long way towards producing software unique in its imaginative qualities, as well as in its deliberate linking with non-computer materials for an overall, unitary approach. The next stage is the problem. Already there is a sense that the more conservative departments will be attracted by electronic Ridout, micro'd Mansfield. Computer suites are being planned with machines permanently established in a small room far away from English and humanities classrooms: hardly a resource available to all. There are anxieties about what machine is the most appropriate: should schools have machines all of one type, or is it possible for an English department to use its own BBC Model B, while the computer studies department works with 380Zs? Interestingly, our teachers' groups are provisionally designing material for BBC machines, but within 24 hours of the decision being made, questions were asked in one school as to the wisdom of it. Elsewhere, most gratifyingly, English departments are developing links with computer studies teachers to their mutual benefit.

It is salutary to look back at the notes of the group's earliest deliberations: there were anxieties about making the materials accessible to the whole ability range. Several teachers insisted that the 'less able' must be able to enjoy and to learn from the experiences devised as readily as the 'bright'. That constraint, if such it is, has been adhered to throughout and there is every reason to hope that the materials produced will be most worthwhile and effective in mixed-ability classes used to working in small groups.

It's not just schools who are at last coming to grips with the vast potential of the microcomputer. I read recently a significant notice pinned on a school's noticeboard. It described computer-assisted learning at the University of Glasgow Medical School: 'Students are presented with "real life" accident or illness situations and are required to make decisions in real time. The computer presents the consequences of their decisions . . .' There's no guarantee of course that the reality is as worthwhile as that sounds, but the principle underpinning that description is the same as that behind the creative 'activities' devised by the Berkshire teachers.

'. . . Increasingly, children will be taught important parts of their syllabus sitting in front of a computer . . . Why 1984 is going to be a good year . . . It's not an Orwellian prophecy come true, it's actually (dare we say it) fun . . .': the double-page spread in *The Sunday Times* contained much more that chills the blood with its bland assumption that computers will reinforce all the most conventional and stagnant attitudes to teaching and learning. It needn't be like that: the machines and their software can be as sensitive, as open-ended as we care to make them. Perhaps it all depends upon which half of the equation you lay the stress — on teaching or learning. In my view, there should only be learners and facilitators of learning. Perhaps that is the most productive environment in which micros in English teaching can flourish and spread.

Putting the computer in its place

Derrick Daines, consultant teacher, Schools Computer Development Centre, Nottingham

When I was a boy before the Second World War, there used to appear a regular advertisement for an author's aid, a sort of do-it-yourself kit for would-be writers. Since even at that age I had visions of writing the novel of the century, I longed to reply to the advertisement, but where on earth was a schoolboy to get the whole pound that the kit cost?

The advertisement reappeared after the war in *Argosy,* a magazine devoted to the short story and featuring many fine writers such as H E Bates and C S Forrester, to name but two. By this time I had left school and started work and managed to save, little by little. I had been frustrated long enough: I bought my postal order, sent it off and waited to become an author.

By return of post I received an envelope that contained a covering letter and three pieces of card. The letter explained how one was to use the kit. 'Each card carries a list of 36 items. Roll two dice and multiply the throws together. This will give you a number 1 to 36. Take the item with this number on card one and roll again . . .' You have the idea. The first item obtained in this way was a character, the second was a location and the third was an artifact, so that one might have (say) a merchant banker at the bottom of a coalmine with a bloodstained box. After that it was up to you; one created the short story out of these elements. They didn't even include the dice.

Years after the bitterness of being swindled had worn off, I came to realize that the idea did have a certain merit as a stimulus to the imagination. Besides that, the experience was an inexpensive lesson in *caveat emptor* and taught me that there is no substitute for the old maxim for writers, 'Seat of the pants on the seat of the chair and don't move until you've written 500 words'.

Many readers will have wondered if the notion of computers aiding writers is nothing more than an updated version of the swindle outlined above. I have had it put to me in very forcible language that the provision of computers in schools is nothing more than a 'great big con-trick'. The young teacher of English who put this to me appeared to be quite serious. He told me that the trick was being perpetrated by manufacturers, aided and abetted by their friends in high places, simply in order to sell more useless computers. He also told me bluntly that he was the one being swindled, both as a taxpayer and as the long-suffering teacher who was expected to put these monstrosities to use.

Does that ring any bells for you? I suppose that perhaps the majority of teachers will find a faint echo of these sentiments within their hearts, but to see it written or to hear it said out loud is to experience an about-turn of feeling. The young man goes too far. If we analyse our feelings carefully we find that deep down we don't really believe these things at all, although we may think them sometimes. As always, we reserve the Englishman's right to grumble.

At least the young man had the grace to agree that if computers are a 'great big con-trick' then they are the biggest con-trick in the entire history of the world, since they involve countless millions of people and every nation. I think that we could also add that it would be impossible to determine who is being 'conned' and who is doing it.

But it is not a swindle. The computer can and does help millions of writers each and every day, in ways undreamed of a mere ten years ago. Perhaps there is the crux of the unease; perhaps it has all come upon us too swiftly. Perhaps — like all adults in every age and clime — we don't like learning new tricks. Perhaps also it would be better for our own peace of mind to admit it and stop creating smokescreens for our true feelings. Let us admit one thing. We are not being swindled.

To be sure, if we wish we could program a computer to do the three-card-trick described, but that does not make the computer itself a swindle. To exorcise a ghost, I once did program my computer to do exactly that. I wrote three lists and had the computer select one at random out of each. [I have recently been guilty of doing the same thing quite independently. A program of mine to do this appeared in *Educational Computing* in November 1982, based on an idea by Don Clark — Ed.] The results were just the same as that old writer's aid. I had a good laugh and took it to school so that the children could share the joke too. To my surprise, the children laughed but went on to say that they would like to try writing stories outlined by the computer, and some of their efforts were quite creditable. I allowed each child long enough by the computer to get an idea that appealed, and shunted them on when I thought they were no longer seeking inspiration but simply wasting time or seeking amusement.

A little later, I came across a program that 'wrote' millions of different science-fiction stories. It started out in a similar fashion, but some selections were programmed to give even more, so that the computer might produce an entire paragraph of plot. We used this one too, but I was far from happy. I felt that this form of stimulus of the imagination was not what I wanted or what the children needed. More, I felt that we were not utilizing the computer properly, or to its best advantage. This was the mid-70s and there were no brains to pick and no previous experience to draw on.

The turning point in my thinking came when I realized that it was a gross error to have the computer 'centre-stage'. The computer is a tool and like any tool its proper place is in the wings. The most important person in the classroom is the teacher and he is there because the children are important; the computer is and should be one more weapon in his armoury, like blackboards, books and pens. It was an error to attempt — even inadvertently — to replace the teacher or part of him by a computer. It was my job to stimulate the imagination of my pupils, and I could not and would not abrogate it to a heap of wires. I might have the computer to help me help the children, but mine was the central position, not its. Besides, when you came right down to it, there was something mechanical about the story-lines; one detected the patterns after a while. Frankly, I think that I was also just plain jealous.

My first attempts at computer usage had been an apprenticeship; now, after my reappraisal of the proper place for the machine in the classroom, it became one long honeymoon — a love-affair that will never end. Just as I never willingly write articles without a wordprocessor, I will never willingly forgo the use of a computer in my classroom — but it stays firmly in the wings.

As an example of what I consider to be a better use of the computer in the teaching of English, let me recount in some detail one example, D & D. D & D is an affectionate shorthand for 'Dungeons and Dragons', a role-playing game that reached England a few years ago. It has become so popular that there are clubs devoted to it and it has given birth to its own press and literature. I am not a devotee myself, although when I first encountered the game about four years ago, I saw that it would have considerable appeal, and especially to the young.

Forget all notions of board games and also of acting games like charades. In a role-playing game the players assume characters and behave in the game within the limitations of those characters. Games can be started at any time — although considerable preparation is necessary — and postponed at the end of a session. Some games have been going for years now and there are even games played by people scattered across the country and who have never met; but I am talking about D & D instead of computing and teaching.

At that time I was the deputy head of a primary school in a mining town. The school was open-plan and the staff formed into team-teaching groups of three of four. In preparation for the game one team held a couple of meetings at which they thrashed out the details, then one prepared a dungeon plan. This was drawn out on graph paper and the sheets stapled together so that each sheet represented a dungeon level, ground level being uppermost. A copy of the plan was made for each teacher, but at all times was kept hidden from the children. Places were marked on the map where there were supposed to be unguarded treasures.

Another member of the team collected dozens of books from all sorts of sources. These books — ranging from Shakespeare to Poe, the Bible to Norse mythology and myths and legends around the world — had one thing in common; they all contained references to monsters, using the word to denote any creature or being unusual, mythical, or out-of-the-ordinary.

When the term began, the children had the game explained to them and had the free choice of persona out of human, elf, dwarf, hobbit or fairy. Then, depending upon the persona chosen, the computer generated numbers representing each person's strength, agility and so on. Each was then given a fixed sum of money with which they could buy useful articles from the shop: articles such as swords, lanterns, rope, water-bottles, knapsacks, daggers, matches — all at fixed prices. The children did not have enough money to buy more than a quarter of the goods on sale, but had to exercise their own judgement on what would be the most useful.

Finally, the children formed themselves into exploration parties of four or five, gave themselves fanciful names and opened diaries. The game began.

One group at a time would be under the supervision of one of the four teachers, with whom they conducted their exploration of the dungeon. The children were given graph paper upon which to build up their own maps of the dungeon and, by consulting his or her own map, the teacher would describe to them what they could see — passageways, doors, stairs, etc — although some items like trapdoors were presumed invisible. Similarly, the teacher would exercise discretion on the range of vision, depending upon whether or not the children had lamps and had remembered to light them.

When the teacher considered that the children had explored far enough for one session, or if another group was ready to start, he or she would announce that a monster had been met. A quick roll of dice, consultation of tables, and the monster was selected.

The group of children now had to find out all that they could about the selected monster and of course this is where the collection of books came into the picture. Each child kept a book of monsters and had to write descriptions as well as draw or paint or make a model. This could be very difficult because the writer often evokes images without actually describing anything. For example, does anyone

34

have a definitive scale-by-scale or feather-by-feather description of a kraken or slithy tove? This sort of problem gave the teachers ample opportunity to discuss and illustrate literary style as well as lead discussions on the origins of some monster myths and legends, etc.

The children were expected to maintain diaries of their explorations; books that gradually grew and grew into novelette proportions. Since the children were 'living' the explorations — making their own decisions, finding their way through unknown territory in a close approximation to the real thing, their writings became more and more vivid, economical and effective. Finally, when all members of the exploration party had finished their assigned work, they presented themselves at the computer. (Ah — I wondered where that was coming in!)

The computer had been programmed quite elaborately. Coded details of the exploration party were fed into it, plus a code number for the monster, and it then went into a blow-by-blow account of the encounter. If, that is, the children elected to attack, for at every stage they were offered choices of action. The monster code number informed the computer of a considerable amount of detail pertaining to the monster — its size and strength, for example, its hostility or friendliness, whether or not it (he? she?) could fly, use magic, what weapons it had, its courage, thickness of hide and how much effort would be required to kill it, so on and so on. Again, the children had to make their own decisions and suffer or gain from the consequences.

When the encounter was concluded — either through the monster or children running away, being 'killed' or befriended — the computer then determined if treasure was found on the body or given as token of friendship, and finally every child was awarded points which went towards promotion, which in turn enabled them to see further, fight better, do magic, discover treasure and so on. Children 'killed' in combat could restart with a new persona, but a careful adjustment of the mathematical model was necessary to strike a nice balance between early discouragement and headstrong behaviour.

At the conclusion of the computer/encounter stage, the children again brought their diaries up to date and then presented themselves back to the teacher for another round of exploration.

The game had other peripheral activities too. Not only was the team richly decorated as a dungeon, with walls and ceilings decked out in painted stonework, added touches of paper chains and papier-mâché monsters, skulls, witches and what-have-you, but other lessons took on a dungeon flavour. Simple cookery included the use of 'ground-up bones' (flour) or 'witches blood' (cochineal) and other renamed ingredients. The music teacher found plenty of suitable songs and music of all kinds, and the PE teacher temporarily renamed favourite games and sports. Once one sets free the imagination of the staff, there is no end to its ingenuity.

It will be observed from the above description that the computer was firmly relegated to a subsidiary — although important — position. It might be asked why one needs the computer at all, but if you think about it, you will realize that this question will always crop up whenever the machine is not back in the very centre of attention — and we know the worries that occur when that happens. On the other hand, the computer in the D & D game was doing something that could be done in no other way. To conduct an interactive encounter of that complexity in any other way whatsoever would have been so time-consuming that it could not have been contemplated. If one had discarded that portion of the game altogether, one would have robbed it of its most exciting aspect, perhaps with fatal results for the project as a whole. The game occupied four teachers and 120 children on most afternoons for a whole term. Interest was so high, creativity and application so great, that the following term all tacitly agreed on a period of slowing down, almost as though rest and relaxation were necessary. After that, demand for other games grew — but that is another story.

Since 1977 the computer market has expanded at a phenomenal rate, as have the capabilities of the computer. Principal improvements have been in memory size, graphics, colour and sound, but none of these in one whit alter the applications that I advocate and which I have exampled, save that writing programs for these machines has become rather more difficult if one wishes to take full advantage of the facilities that they offer. Personally, I believe that the classroom would become very noisy if one had machines beeping and warbling all around the place, so I tend to be very sparing with sound effects, and any handiman could quickly disable the internal speaker if the teacher found that necessary. On the other hand, computer graphics—especially in colour—are tremendously useful and exciting, offering ways of capturing the imagination that are just beginning to be explored.

Taken in real terms, the £1 that I was swindled out of in 1945 would have been worth £15 or so today. For a considerably smaller sum one may buy a tape of computer programs, each of which can stimulate the imaginations of our pupils enormously. Let us grasp the opportunity with both hands.

36

A world in a grain of sand

Don Clark, adult education tutor, Leeds

I am just old enough to have used an inkwell and dip-pen at school. I remember the rise of the fountain pen and the brief opposition to the inexorable biro. English teaching has come a long way since the wax tablet, slate and quill. Some English departments have cassette-recorders! But in this article I will concern myself, and perhaps concern you, with the teaching of writing.

'We sit and write, we sit and write, we sit and write;
All our lessons we sit and write.
WE SIT AND WRITE.
WHY DO WE SIT AND WRITE?'

Because, Ruth Dyer aged 11, English is a poorly financed, exam-orientated, service subject. Ruth typed her poem at home.

At one of the several adult education centres in which I now work there is a typewriter available for adult literacy students to use. They do so frequently. What they gain, in terms of presentation, precision and the stimulus of a new medium, seems to more than outweigh their painfully slow progress with the unfamiliar keyboard. Ruth must have thought so too. But, since the first mass-produced typewriters were introduced by Remington & Sons in 1874, teachers of English have failed to answer the challenge and realize the potential of this new technology. Perhaps the following difficulties discouraged them from making typing facilities available to students of English. Firstly, the finance and the fuss; secondly, students' lack of keyboard familiarity, and lastly the inflexibility of typed text and the difficulty of revision...

I am not writing, as I have had to do in the past, on a piece of paper. If I had been it would already be covered with crossings-out, tiny spiralling strands of rubber, fingermarks and creases. Thank goodness. Should the person from Porlock arrive I would hate to have to return to that! I am not using a typewriter either. Had I done so the page would have been rapidly overwritten with X's and Tipp-Ex until there was no further room for corrections and the page was either retyped or ripped out of the typewriter and set upon with pencil or pen. Of, if I had quailed at the thought of so thorough a purge, I might have spent the entire article dredging up arguments to justify the existence of its opening lines. Fortunately I have access to a wordprocessor, and so my integrity as a writer need not be diminished!

The Government has coughed up the cash to provide schools with computers, and many computers make excellent wordprocessors. A computer by itself is useless for anything besides computing, but put a program into its memory and it becomes a tool, or a stimulus, or a resource, or a game. Feed it with a wordprocessing program and it will become all of these. So what is a wordprocessor? I will begin by describing a program designed for students to use.

1. The word-processing program is stored on a cassette-tape.
2. Once this has been fed into the computer by a cassette-recorder the program can begin.
3. The program may display its title or a screen of helpful information, after which the screen can be cleared for writing.
4. The screen becomes blank, except for a cursor (a block or line that indicates where the next letter will be written).
5. The cursor can be moved to any position on the screen by pressing the keys marked with arrows.
6. Text can be overwritten by new text or deleted by pressing the DELETE key.
7. The adjustable tabulator, shift and carriage return facilities are similar to those of typewriters. But, because there is no moving carriage, when the cursor reaches the end of a line it reappears conveniently at the beginning of the next line.
8. The key marked CTRL (control), when pressed at the same time as a letter key, allows quick and easy access to a number of functions and writing modes.
9. There is an 'insert' mode where existing text will move or make room for new words, or to close up unwanted gaps.
10. The 'copy' mode allows text to be edited as it is copied from one part of the screen to another.
11. Lines of text can be moved or removed instantaneously.
12. At the bottom of the screen beneath the text there is a space for helpful information about modes and options.
13. Writing can be interrupted at any time — to view a complete 'page' of helpful information — and resumed with ease.
14. There is space available for more text than would fit on the screen, so each page (or screenful) of text has a number. Selecting a different page is like push-button channel selection on a TV.
15. Sections of text can be copied from one page to another.
16. Pages can be quickly cleared of text.
17. There is a facility for examining all the pages as if they were all winding or unwinding from scrolls at the top and bottom of the screen.

18. Pages can be recorded on cassette-tape and recordings can be checked.
19. Previously recorded pages can be retrieved from cassette-tape for display, further editing or inclusion in new text.
20. Pages can be printed out when a printer is available.
21. Some facilities, such as taping, can be applied to several pages at a time.
22. When special function keys are pressed, previously prepared words and phrases can be rapidly added to the text, to save repetitive typing.
23. Coloured, flashing and extra-large lettering can be displayed.

A wordprocessing program such as this would be inexpensive — about £10 — and would take two minutes to load from a cassette-recorder into the computer. Students could use it to create stories, poems and poster displays, for functional, descriptive and discursive, writing, for editing previously prepared text and for games such as 'Consequences'. A wordprocessor provides as many possibilities as a pen with the additional advantages of clarity, compelling redrafting facilities and the fascination of a screen medium.

Screen-reading and keyboard skills are already important (and will be essential) elements of communication and information-gathering. There are already several alternatives to the traditional QWERTY keyboard, and primitive speech-synthesising and speech-recognition devices are already commercially available. Nevertheless the QWERTY keyboard, with all its imperfections, will be with us for many years to come, and will probably never be completely superseded. My experience of students who have used typewriters suggests that keyboard work can be beneficial for non-typists. But I suspect that the keyboard habits acquired in this way may disrupt the development of efficient typing techniques later.

The cheap Sinclair Spectrum computer, one of several recommended for use in primary schools by the DES, lacks a proper keyboard. Secondary schools can therefore expect a flood of squinting, knuckle typists. Computer studies does not teach typing. If you try out the keyboard familiarity programs supplied with the BBC and Spectrum computers you will discover that these are only tests. Computer manufacturers avoid the question of typing skills. Advertisements show confident computer owners with one finger poised above the keyboard. There was a time when I typed with only one finger — and a very long time it took. The teaching of typing in primary schools is long overdue, and is likely to remain so. The teaching of office skills in secondary schools will change because it must. There are now far fewer vacancies for typists, most office equipment will be microelectronic and the skills expected of office workers will be more sophisticated. Office skills, as a subject available in schools, will probably disappear. I would like to float the suggestion that office skills should be expanded to teach keyboard skills to all students. Furthermore, as typing involves close attention to form, I suggest that English relinquish its role as a service subject and hand over punctuation, grammar and spelling to office skills. English can concern itself with the content of communication, with style, language, literature... but always with style.

English departments have yet to claim their right to use typewriters and computers. There is no need to wait until students arrive in class fully equipped with keyboard skills. If English teachers do this they may find themselves in a position similar to that of the Latin teachers who confused the relevance of linguistics and Roman literature with the irrelevance of a complex word puzzle. Language lives, and means of expression change, so English as a subject must adjust. If a student prefers screen viewing to book reading (or *vice versa*) then English should respond to that interest and present alternatives.

I have described some of the facilities which wordprocessors have for the revision of text and I have discussed some of the problems involved in the introduction of keyboard work. I have suggested a means of reducing the burden upon English teachers so that they would have time to develop the uses of new technology. The final question will be that of finance.

It would be trivial to argue that a wordprocessor is superior to paper and pen or a typewriter or *vice versa*. I use all three. As teachers we are in the business of offering alternatives. Wordprocessors are going to play a part in education. They are already an essential element in the teaching of office skills, they will be used for administration in school offices and they will probably be exhibited during computer studies. But what a waste! The practical equipment which should be the province of the English department disappears into the office skills section, reprographics, and now (since computers are still associated with meaningless symbols and mad scientists) the maths and science departments. Imagine art as a subject in which practical graphics work was limited to the use of charcoal pencils (or, worse still, biros), or music with mouth-organs. Computers are particularly efficient at manipulating words and students have the potential to manipulate meanings. They really ought to get together during English lessons.

Information retrieval is already the province of English, it comes under the category of reference skills. Screen-reading is part of a new literacy — computer literacy — but the expertise required to teach it is outside the field of computer studies. Typewriters and wordprocessors are essential in the teaching of English. They have not been available because English teachers have decided that they will not be made available. It is not necessary to ask for this equipment, it will be sufficient merely to state that it is needed . . . and to refuse to accept that there are grounds for denial. Meanwhile sufficient finance has already been provided to allow English departments the occasional use of wordprocessors, and amongst their hardworking staff will be some who are enthusiastic, energetic, conscientious or curious enough to try them out.

One wordprocessor is better than none. Its use could be shared between students, but its screen display makes it particularly suitable for group-work. Texts for further revision, and completed work, can be stored on cassette-tapes. Schools and colleges may share printer facilities, but a printout will not always be a necessary (or even desirable) addition to an already attractive presentation on a screen.

When a word is written, typed or keyed in, the writer will hopefully become aware of its implications, associations and alternatives. As more words are added these are controlled, until, in the final text, the intended meanings are clear and unambiguous. It is not always possible to predict implications, associations and alternatives before words are written; hence the importance of drafts. Students are often reluctant to rewrite drafts, but a wordprocessor is designed to make this easy. It stimulates creativity by encouraging experimentation with words and, therefore, with ideas. On a wordprocessor, the implications, associations and alternatives that each new word suggests will be controlled, but they won't be lost. Those possibilities will remain open for as long as the text remains on the screen. And, when the screen is cleared again, the possibilities will become almost infinite — a world of possibilities, in a grain of sand.

New machines for old mechanics?

George Keith, Director, Cheshire Language Centre

By the 1970s the century-old running battle between English literature and the Industrial Revolution had just about run out of steam. To teachers of English the old entrenchments and battlelines are familiar enough: personal craftmanship versus mass production, books versus moving pictures, men versus machines, nostalgia versus contemporary culture (though it is noticeable that during the seventies the media cultivated images of the past, very successfully making them thoroughly modern and extremely profitable).

Microprocessors have created a new social revolution and the educational use of computers may well seem a last straw to those teachers who have never really come to terms with machines in the classroom. The knowing smile when the taperecorder goes wrong persists as a justification for not really having wanted to entrust the lesson to a machine in the first place. Many teachers stolidly refuse to use the resources of video for anything more adventurous than watching playbacks, and whilst the 16mm projector is admittedly becoming a thing of the past, an extraordinary number of teachers have managed to maintain a deliberately ham-fisted ignorance about how to operate one. Perhaps, with the spread of computers in the classroom, there will be a 'back to the 16mm projector' movement spearheaded by teachers who never used one very much in the first place.

The main purpose of this paper is to suggest that by the imaginative construction and use of English language learning programs, teachers will not be capitulating to a new technology but may actually rescue English language teaching from ineffective mechanistic approaches that have been with us for so long and which are less mechanistic simply for having been produced in textbooks as opposed to computer software.

Before considering actual programs for language development, it may be of interest to recount some of the thinking that lies behind a research project jointly proposed by the Cheshire Language Centre and the North West Regional Computer Centre at North Cheshire College.

Learning grammar and learning to write
'Considering how painlessly children learn to talk, the difficulties they face in writing are quite pronounced. Indeed, some children never learn to write at all, and many fall far short of full proficiency

in the skills of writing. It seems from this that there is more involved in the learning of writing than fairly mechanical translation skills.'[1]

The spectre of Gradgrind is frequently invoked to warn us of a new utilitarianism, a new faith in technology that will enslave the human spirit more than ever before. In Dickens' novel *Hard Times*, the value of human life is expressed in terms of a man's 'hands' and the labour those hands can perform in mines and factories. The image of hands also extends to the 'statistical clock' telling the time in Gradgrind's study. An ironist may well find a modern counterpart to this in the word 'digits', signifying not only numbers on an LED digital display, but also fingers that flick across computer keyboards endlessly programming information and instruction.

The differences between men and machines, between the arts and the sciences, may not be glossed over lightly and it is singularly unhelpful if they become polarized. Nor are English teachers by any means united on one side or the other. The experience of many suggests an uncomfortable state of tension between the two perspectives.

What should be emphasized though is that the mechanistic approach, far from being an external threat to the teaching of English, has long existed within. There is no doubt that many children's experience of literature has suffered at the hands of mechanistic and unimaginative teaching, but the real casualty has been English language, that neglected other half of English teaching which is also, along with numeracy, the oldest subject in the school curriculum.

The notion that children learn best by drills and the naming of parts has woefully afflicted the teaching of English language so much so that grammar has become a thing of ill repute. It seems to do nobody any observable good and in the sixties we were heartily grateful of excuses to forget about grammar altogether and concentrate on creative writing. Mechanistic approaches to grammar have however continued to appear in publishers' lists, they are still being bought by both primary and secondary schools and the contemporary 'back to basics' cry is a strong one in some quarters. In spirit of course that kind of 'basic' could not be further removed from the possibilities offered by use of the computer language of the same name. But that is yet another irony.

Grammatical understanding, both intuitive and reflective, is essential for achievement in writing because it relates the ways in which we think to the ways in which we express ourselves with the written word. It is in the area of these grammatical links between thinking and writing that interesting possibilities for computer programs occur. Writing of any kind is frequently a lonely, unsupported task yet it is enmeshed in a network of psychological and social influences that make instruction extremely difficult. Problems of style and syntax are equally difficult for both learners and teachers. They cause headaches and heart-searching and so much of an English teacher's time is spent attending to the effects of children not saying what they think they are saying, or in trying to read for meaning between the lines. All this is a common responsibility and it was oddly reassuring to learn from one interviewer that even Marshall McLuhan, herald of a new technological − linguistic revolution, spent his days in the routine of marking English essays.

We know that important stages of grammatical learning can be seen in children's writing between the ages of about nine and thirteen, but we also know that the writing abilities of large numbers of children appear to develop very little in the secondary school years. The discouraging effect of this can be seen in the performance of O-level English language candidates who consistently fail to achieve a fair standard in successive items of Mode 3 course work and who will predictably fail written papers because of syntactic and stylistic inadequacies.

The teaching of writing, if it is to help children who would otherwise underachieve, must foster grammatical intuition and reflection and it may well succeed in doing this by paying explicit attention to syntactical aspects of writing.

Self-help in writing
One of the ways in which young writers may be taught to help each other is by the formation of small groups, of about four to six, willing to discuss each other's writing in some detail. Many of the social factors influencing writing (eg, audience and register) may be examined in this way and frequently the more personal question of stylistic maturity is also raised.

One criterion of immaturity, usually recognized by teachers and only dimly perceived by students, is the recurrence of short, subject − verb − object sentences that have the overall effect of preventing writers from saying what they want to say and of shunting their thoughts into what the writers themselves do not find particularly interesting. Short sentences are not in principle unsatisfactory, but if they limit a writer's powers of expression the responsive teacher is left to read between the lines once again and the examiner will inevitably find it difficult to give marks to what is in effect a series of shortcircuits.

Self-help groups are able to correct most spelling, punctuation and common grammatical errors collectively without any reference to a teacher, but two areas in which they need to turn to a teacher are:

(i)   vocabulary, ie, finding the 'right' word
(ii) syntax, ie, making more explicit the connections and relationships between ideas.

Group discussion provides vital opportunities for learning about purposes and audiences for writing, and about the effects of the language produced, but in the process of sharing experience each member is made conscious of areas of reflective language learning which must be developed (or trained) at a personal level. A serious comment from one 16-year-old, 'I know what I mean but I can't put it into words', or a joking comment like 'I can do joined-up writing but I'm not so good at joined-up thinking', indicate the measure of difficulty. The instinctive recognition however, of the importance of lexical choice and syntactic construction, points to specific learning needs that teachers could constructively and usefully develop if the right kind of resource for individual learning were available.

The North Cheshire Project: 'Primary language programs'
Various attempts at explicit grammar teaching (chiefly by use of workcards) have been investigated at the Cheshire Language Centre and in particular comparisons have been made of grammatical constructions produced in speech with those produced in writing. Interesting as this has been, there remains the difficulty of finding the right kind of manageable individual instruction that would relate to each student's natural use of language. An unexpected invitation however, from the North West Regional Computer Centre suggested a new way forward and resulted in the Centre collaborating on 'Primary language programs', a project based at North Cheshire College and financed by MEP. This has given an opportunity to investigate language use by younger children alongside continuing study of less able O-level candidates, though it is already becoming evident that the programs devised will be equally useful in secondary schools in view of the differential rates of development that take place in language learning and the need for many students to return to earlier stages — like the gardener's advice to beginners wishing to plant rose bushes, 'First dig a trench ten years ago!' The four programs in preparation focus on two areas of language learning:

(i)   lexical choice
(ii) sentence-joining.

These correspond to two generally recognized dimensions of language use: (i) the theoretically infinite range of lexical choice facing a writer which may be represented vertically with each new

46

word chosen (the paradigmatic dimension) and (ii) the succession of words linked by linear or horizontal structures (the syntagmatic dimension).

The class or function of each word chosen will of course be determined by the syntactic structure that is being generated in the sentence.

Lexical choice: synonyms

The notion that children's 'word power' may be increased by learning decontextualized lists of words (or even lists derived from texts recently read) is a limited one. Such lists may well contribute to the store of latent words that children may be said to know but it remains just as difficult to tap that store for personal spontaneous use in writing. There may be a value in drawing children's attention to words for their own sake, but unless there is a follow-up activity in which they are required to put the words into groups or find relationships with other words it is difficult to know what to do with new words in isolation. Adding to the word-hoard seems to be most profitable if it is done by a conscious searching for words with which to achieve specific ends.

Roget's Thesaurus and other synonym dictionaries are well known attempts to provide writers with immediate assistance when searching for a word but they seem to be most helpful to writers well on the way to being able to help themselves and least helpful to inexperienced writers. Choices in a thesaurus are frequently outside the range of experience of young writers or too abstract.

A computer word-bank of synonyms can quite easily be devised but it does not function in any way that is essentially different from a dictionary or thesaurus. The aim of 'Primary language programs' is to construct programs on lexical choice that will follow the writer's search for words and instruct him or her what to do next. The stimulus to search for an alternative word comes in the first instance from a responsive reader (teacher, parent, other pupil) and should arise in the context of a piece of writing done as part of normal classwork or for homework.

Initially the word-bank is empty and the computer is programmed to give instruction on how to search for alternative words and check them in a class dictionary. These are then fed into the word-bank where sets of synonyms are gradually built up, devised from children's own word searches and embodying discriminations they themselves have made. As the word-bank grows it provides unique data about children's personal use of, and reflection upon, words and their meanings. If the computer is later unable to supply a choice of synonyms it instructs the user how to increase its store so that a group of pupils or a whole class may in the course of say two terms build its own data-bank and in the process develop its own power to search for words. A later stage of programming will make use of information in the data-bank as a basis for activities in classification and thinking about creative uses of words.

Syntax: making sentences make sense

The chief disadvantage of textbook exercises in syntax have been that the activities prescribed use decontextualized words and work only on the surfaces of sentences. Consequently the learning that takes place does not usually affect the varieties of relational thinking that actually produce or generate complex sentences. Argument has raged for many years over the value of explicit grammar teaching and its effects upon the development of children's writing abilities. It is not difficult to see that knowing how to analyse a sentence into its immediate constituent parts does not transfer automatically to knowing how to write continuous, complex statements that are forming in the mind. What seems to be needed in the classroom today is a range of new activities designed to stimulate personal thinking of a relational kind rather than computerized sets of old-fashioned drills in the manipulation of other people's sentences. Once again the use of machines may be as mindless or as inventive as the program will allow.

A starting point for looking at relational thinking and syntactic structures lies in the use of prepositions. These words lie comfortably within the knowledge of nine-year-olds but are fundamental to thinking at any level. With the aid of computer graphics it is possible to move from the perception of diagrammatic relationships to the expression of those relationships verbally. A flexible program works both ways, requiring users to formulate explicit instructions using appropriate prepositions. Just as in thought, so in a computer program prepositions function as signals directing the reader's attention to specific locations. Programs devised by the North Cheshire Project aim to encourage the greatest possible flexibility in choosing and locating prepositions, for experience has shown that the inventiveness of children engaged in activities of this kind defies the use of prescribed grammatical labels. It is also noticeable that any extended work on prepositions leads naturally into a consideration of adverbs and adverbial phrases, especially when there is an attempt to relate objects, events or ideas in time as well as space.

The other major area of syntax with which 'Primary language programs' is concerned is sentence-joining and the appropriate use of subordinating conjunctions. Researchers such as William Harpin[2] at Nottingham, and Katherine Perera[3] at Manchester University, have already given teachers valuable guidance about the development and use of subordination by children. Some American researchers have also investigated sentence-combining as a way of tapping not only what students already know about language but don't necessarily produce, but also of following more closely the natural ways in which clauses and sentences are produced and ordered. The conclusion of Stanley Straw, for example, that sentence-combining activities 'because they are based on and expand the language ability of students and because of the synthetic nature of the activities, significantly affect productive and receptive language growth'[4] accords with a study of O-level English language students needing special attention with their reading and writing.

A simple form of sentence-joining program consists of one set of subordinating conjunctions (eg, although, whenever, unless, because) together with a set of simple sentences to be joined in combinations of two (or later) three.

This program can be used by individuals, pairs of children or by small groups and requires users to make judgements about the sense or nonsense of different combinations. The guiding principle is not to find correct answers but to consider the variety of possibilities that make sense.

Examples of combination (permissible or otherwise) that might appear on the screen are:

I am wearing my wellington boots because it is raining.
Because it is raining I am wearing my wellington boots.
Although it is raining I am wearing my wellington boots.
It is raining because I am wearing my wellington boots.
Whenever it is raining I am wearing my wellington boots.
I am wearing my wellington boots unless it is raining.
Unless it is raining, I am wearing my wellington boots.
It is raining I am wearing my wellington boots because.

The ensuing discussion about the sense or nonsense of different combinations and the flexibility of thinking required to produce alternative combinations demonstrates quire a degree of logical thinking and demands a reflective use of language. A more advanced program is being considered that will use graphics to stimulate language production requiring appropriate uses of subordination.

The most difficult task of all will be devising a means of testing what effects, if any, this kind of language learning will have on children's performance when asked to write in the normal course of school lessons or for homework.

'Primary language programs' in action

'Primary language programs' is a modest proposal for making a start on new approaches to two aspects of language learning in the 9 – 13 age-range. It is too early yet to report usefully on classroom use but some guidelines have already emerged.

(i) Close integration of group-learning approaches with the use of computer programs is desirable and might even provide more point and purpose to collaborative learning than has often been the case.
(ii) Programs should provide opportunities for children to use their own words and should be adaptable to their own purposes however difficult that may make the programming in the first instance. Above all children should be able to make meanings out of what they are doing.
(iii) The opportunities for immediate feedback and self-assessment by the user should not only assist a child's thinking while actually trying to solve a problem or achieve an end but should also provide cumulative data on progress in specific areas of language use.
(iv) Data stored by the computer should be a guide to the teacher in prescribing new directions or further developments in language and learning.

Underlying these guidelines is an optimism that the use of computers in English will change both learning and teaching perceptions of what language is and how it works. Already the use of computers has given literacy a new meaning. Not only do programs, such as the ones outlined here, require a degree of reflection while writing, but the new visual aspects of arranging and rearranging sentences and paragraphs on the display screen also gives a fresh insight into constructional aspects of written English. This paper began with a reference to the grim, mechanistic mind of Mr Gradgrind, the man of facts. There is, however, a wiser, more humane teacher in *Hard Times* often overlooked — Mr Sleary, the circus owner. One of his maxims is an apt text for those starting to use computer programs in English lessons: 'Bring out the best in us, sir, not the worst'.

References
1. KRESS, GUNTHER, *Learning to Write,* Routledge and Kegan Paul, 1982
2. HARPIN, WILLIAM, *The Second 'R',* Allen and Unwin, 1976
3. PERERA, KATHERINE, in *Linguistics and the Teacher* edited by R Carter, Routledge and Kegan Paul, 1982
4. STRAW, STANLEY, in *Research in the Language Arts: language and schooling,* edited by Victor Froese and Stanley B Straw, University Park Press, 1981.

A construction kit for language

Mike Sharples, Department of Artificial Intelligence, Edinburgh University

A tenet of artificial intelligence research is that models are valuable learning aids. A good way to understand the laws, constraints, styles and possibilities of a complex rule-governed system is to build models of the system, subject to the same rules, and then perform experiments on them. Thus, robots provide information on human limb movement and chess-playing computer programs contribute to our understanding of human problem-solving. A child with a Meccano set, who builds a bridge, runs a toy car over it, notices that the bridge sags and so strengthens it with a triangular brace, is carrying out the same process of building and testing models. In the classroom, model-building of this type is generally confined to science and mathematics but, given the right tools, modelling could usefully be extended to other subjects. Imagine a computer program that allows a child to design planets. It would be constrained by the natural laws (although a child who really wants to play God could alter these) so the child would position the planet at the correct distance from the sun to support life, set a size sufficient to hold an atmosphere and so on — then send the planet spinning into orbit and observe it over the next million years. The program need be no more complicated to operate than a video game, yet it would help the child to understand not only *what* are the important aspects of geography, physics and ecology but also *why* they are important.

Unfortunately, no planet-building program exists, yet, but computer programs of similar sophistication have been developed over the past decade to model another complex system-language. My intention has been to adapt some of these programs, sacrificing their power or flexibility, for use by children.

To give an example, one aim of research in linguistics is to build computer models of generative grammars — programs that can generate well-formed sentences, poems or stories. POEM is a child's version of generative grammar.

POEM

The child begins by creating 'silly stories'. The program has an inbuilt library of 'story patterns' and the child can call one up by typing 'get' and then the name of the pattern (Figure 1). A story then builds up on the screen but at various points the program stops and requests the child to type in a word to continue the story (Figure 2).

51

Each word that the child contributes is printed on the screen and also stored in POEM's 'vocabulary', according to part of speech. If, instead of typing a word, the child presses the 'space' bar, then the program chooses a word of the correct part of speech, at random, from its vocabulary (Figure 4). (After a few stories the vocabulary fills up so the child can just keep pressing 'space' and allow the program to fill in the blanks.) The program makes no check on the words entered, so if a child types 'runs' in response to 'TYPE AN ADVERB' then 'runs' is stored as an adverb. However, the child soon realizes the problem when the program generates sentences like 'Mrs Sproggs sits runs on the sofa'.

GET story pattern PATTERN: story 1

Figure 1

The start of a 'silly story' (words typed by the child are underlined)

This is a tale about a
GET story pattern PATTERN: story 1 TYPE AN ADJECTIVE: stupid

Figure 2

The program asks for an adjective.

This is a tale about a STUPID called Mr
GET story pattern PATTERN: story 1 TYPE A NAME Sproggs

Figure 3

The program asks for a name

This is a tale about a STUPID called Mr SPROGGS who lives in a TINY house with a GERBIL and a FEROCIOUS CAT. He often EATS SLOWLY as he is extremely TINY
GET story pattern PATTERN: story 1 TYPE AN ADJECTIVE:

Figure 4

The child responds by pressing 'space' so the program selects an adjective at random-in this case 'TINY.

The next stage is for the child to create her own story patterns. She types 'get' and then, instead of giving the name of a story, she types in a pattern, for example:

PATTERN: Mr name is a very adjective man.

Once the pattern (which can be as long as the child wishes) has been entered,the program prints out the story, generating a word at random for each part of speech, for example:

Mr Sproggs is a very ferocious man.

Another command, 'put', allows the child to add words directly to the vocabulary and so create more complex patterns, for example:

PUT words in to the vocabulary
PART OF SPEECH: nounphrase
WORDS: the adjective noun
PART OF SPEECH: nounphrase
WORDS: the noun
PART OF SPEECH: sentence
WORDS: nounphrase verb nounphrase

With these rules in store the program can be given the pattern 'sentence' and will generate, for example:

The gerbil eats the tiny cat.

Finally, patterns can be designed which ask for responses from the user, like those in Figures 1-4, and can be added to the program's library.

Through building models of language with the POEM program a child can develop an active understanding of parts of speech and sentence construction. Grammar is no longer a set of disembodied textbook exercises, but the means to create funny stories.

POEM is one of a suite of programs for language exploration. One, GRAM 3 allows the child not only to specify sentence patterns, but also to match words and phrases for meaning. Another, WALTER (WORD ALTERER) lets the child study grammatical transformations on text. She can type a story to the program and then see the effect of, for example, deleting every occurrence of a selected part of speech, changing a sentence from active to passive voice, or combining sentences. A standard WALTER rule is 'relative' which combines sentences using relative clauses. The child types in, for example:

Once there was a pretty princess. The princess lived in a big castle in a forest. The forest was dark. She was very lonely because she had no friends to play with.

She then types the command 'relative' and WALTER changes the text to:

Once there was a pretty princess who lived in a big castle in a dark forest. She was very lonely because she had no friends to play with.

Language kit
Together, the programs form a construction kit for language, very similar in concept to Meccano kits for engineering. The child starts by following construction plans, or by building her own simple and unwieldy structures from a small set of parts. Then, as she learns about the properties of the parts and the constraints of the system, she can create more sophisticated models. Finally, she can combine the simple parts into sub-assemblies (with Meccano a pulley system or trolley, with POEM a phrase or sentence) which can then be used as the building units for complex and realistic structures.

The programs have been used by 11-year-old children to create silly stories, by two 15-year-old boys who wrote grammars for a prototype of GRAM 3 that generated thematic poems, and by students of linguistics. As tools rather than teaching aids the programs are not tied to a particular syllabus and, since the words and grammar are supplied by the user, they can be used to manipulate any language — from Latin to BASIC.

Creative writing
Language play is a worthwhile activity in itself. A child can develop reasoning skills, an understanding of literary style, and an appreciation of language. However, the language kit was originally designed to serve an ulterior need: to help children make the difficult transition from speech-like writing to mature creative composition. Research in children's writing development (Bereiter and Scardamalia, 1982) indicates that creative writing is not a simple extension of speech, but a major reconstruction. In order to write successfully, for a variety of functions and audiences, the child must understand the writing process — of idea creation, planning, text production and text revision. She must learn to produce language without the aid of conversational cues and to communicate with an unknown audience in text that has a well-turned form and an elegant style. A good writer can separate language from its immediate context, so that it becomes an object to be shaped and polished. Such linguistic knowledge is very different from the initial awareness of language needed for conversation.

This has clear implications for the teaching of creative writing. It suggests that a child should progress from 'spilling thoughts on to paper' towards an understanding of the process of writing. Idea creation, story planning and text revision should be as important to this process as text production. Teaching schemes for creative writing generally have little to say about planning and revision of text, which is not surprising given that these are still poorly understood aspects of language, and also that pen and paper are exceedingly poor tools for the job. A child is understandably loath to deface her neatly written story with messy deletions and insertions; she is equally reluctant to rewrite it all just to improve the style of one section.

Writing aids
Computer programs can break the bond between word and paper, providing a new medium for writing, whereby text can be planned, formed and altered with equal ease. WALTER, the text transforming program, is also the prototype of a writing aid for children. It acts as a simple wordprocessor, with only two basic commands — 'new' and 'change'. After typing 'new' the child can input text as if using a typewriter. The 'change' command is used to make any alterations to the text, from a spelling correction to a grammatical transformation. Incorporated into the program is a thesaurus, that can be called by typing the command 'thesaurus':

thesaurus
WORD TO BE LOOKED UP: big
big: large, huge, gigantic, giant, massive, important

WALTER is one step towards a computer-based 'writer's assistant'. Other steps have been taken elsewhere. The STORY MAKER program, developed by Andee Rubin (Rubin, 1980), allows children to explore alternative story structures in order to develop their skills of story planning, and the WRITER'S WORKBENCH produced by Bell Labs is a growing selection of programs attached to a word-processor and designed to aid a writer by, for example, checking for possible spelling errors, poor punctuation and 'awkward or wordy phrases'.

Teaching scheme
By themselves the computer programs are insufficient as teaching aids and so they have been combined with written worksheets to form a self-study course on language and creative writing. The course is in two sections. The first develops a child's understanding of language, through exercises and games — some using the

computer, some, such as a sentence version of Scrabble and a grammar crossword, for pencil and paper. This gives a foundation to the second part of the course in which the child applies knowledge to creative writing through a series of writing projects. A pilot version of the scheme has been tested with six 11-year-old children who visited Edinburgh University for 2-4 hours per week over two school terms. The section below describes a series of worksheets from the second part of the course concerned with descriptive writing.

Descriptive writing
The children began the section by playing language games designed to expand their range of descriptive words and phrases. One game made use of a program which substitutes an asterisk for an adjective and an exclamation mark for an adverb. As the computer only recognizes some 200 words, the aim of the game is to 'outwit' the machine by inventing sentences with unusual modifiers that will not be substituted by the program. The children were provided with core sentences, which they then embellished; for example, 'The man sat on the bench'.

get
PATTERN: The old grey-haired man
PATTERN: sat sadly on the uneven
PATTERN: green bench.
The * grey-haired man sat ! on the uneven * bench.

To break the children from their normal clutch of uninspired modifiers — 'big', 'nasty', 'horrible', etc — the online thesaurus offered them synonyms of common words.
  A series of exercises then developed their skills in writing simple descriptions. In one exercise a group of children wrote a description of an unusual picture. This was passed to another group who attempted to redraw the picture guided only by the written text.

FANTASY
The final part was a project in which the children built up descriptions first into a written environment and then into a story with the aid of a program named FANTASY. They were split into two groups. Each group drew up a plan of an imaginary house, with rooms, connecting doors, and secret passages. The group then wrote descriptions of each room, plus details of treasure and the occupants of the house.
  One group of children asked if they could write the descriptions on their own. They arrived the next week with eight sides of A4 filled

with information about the house. The children all typed their descriptions to the computer, using the WALTER program, and these, along with details of the room layout, were incorporated into the FANTASY program (they were given assistance with the final stage of indicating the logic of the room layout in a form suitable for the program) which was then ready to be used as a game. They swapped programs and each group 'explored' the opponent's house, fought off the inhabitants and found the treasure, by typing commands to the program. Below is the start of a game session. The design of the house and the descriptions of rooms, characters, and treasure were devised entirely by the children (game commands are underlined).

Welcome to FANTASY

You are in a long straight hallway with brown oak walls, hanging on the walls are old Victorian pictures. On the ground is telephone table and chair.

a wooden door leads south
a front door leads east

South
You are in a blue coloured bedroom, with a mysterious atmosphere. There is a strange rattling noise coming from the window. In the bedroom there is a toilet which is at the left-hand corner.There is a chest of drawers and a wardrobe to match. In front of the bed there is a grey, wet mist.

a wooden door leads north
a wooden door leads west

a chef has just arrived through a wooden door (west)

Objects
you can see
1 — a gold bracelet and earrings to match
2 — a bottle of wine

The role of FANTASY was to aid the children in moving from static descriptions into dynamic narrative. After playing the game the children discussed their experiences and this led them to an examination of goals (the goal of the explorer is to find the hidden treasure and the goal of the inhabitants is to attack the intruder) and strategies (one way to play the game is to stay in a room, wait until people arrive in it with treasure and then attack them!), in narrative writing and of the interaction between description and plot (houses with secret passages and hidden treasure demand more complex exploration strategies and so increase suspense). The children then wrote adventure stories based on their experiences of playing FANTASY.

Conclusion
The pilot project indicated no single teaching strategy or method of use — some children tired of the computer after five minutes, others worked happily for an hour or more; some preferred to work alone at a computer terminal, others used the computer in pairs or groups; some worked smoothly without help, others demanded constant attention and advice. This was expected. The computer programs were not intended to replace or relieve the teacher, nor to fit really into a school curriculum. They do not present a well-defined and examinable set of facts. They were designed to give a child the experience of a research worker, with control over the content and structure of his learning, tools to carry out worthwhile experiments, and equipment to draft and revise the results.

The best location for such a language workshop is a resource centre, with books and audio-visual materials as well as computers, where children can plan their own study and adults are available as advisers – more like a children's library than a classroom. The pilot project suggests that children can learn to control and extend their written language in such an environment, and enjoy the experience.

Acknowledgements
I should like to thank the children of class Primary 7, South Bridge School, Edinburgh, and their teacher Mrs Finlayson, for all their cooperation. I am grateful also to Dr Jim Howe and Dr Ben DuBouley for their supervision of the project and to the Social Science Research Council for financial support.

References
BEREITER, C and SCARDAMALIA, M, from 'Conversation to Composition: the role of instruction in a developmental process', in R Glaser (ed) *Advances in Instructional Psychology,* Vol 2, Lawrence Erlbaum Associates, Hillsdale N J, 1982

FRASE, L T, 'Computer Aids for Text Editing and Design', papers presented at the annual meeting of the American Educational Research Association, Boston, April 1980, Bell Laboratories, Piscataway, N J, 1980.

RUBIN, ANDEE *Making Stories, Making Sense,* Bolt Beranek and Newman Inc, Cambridge, Mass, 1980

Does the use of the microcomputer inhibit the development of language in children?

Jan Stewart, Investigations on Teaching with Microcomputers as an Aid Collaboration

As the use of microcomputers spreads into all types of schools, and all areas of the curriculum, many teachers are expressing concern about its possible effects on the language development of children. Most fears result from a lack of knowledge concerning the purpose and potential of the machines. Images of children sitting in front of screens with glazed vacant eyes or being programmed blindly through sections of a predetermined curriculum are not uncommon nor, if we are truthful, without some foundation. Many teachers will remember links between computers and teaching machines in the fifties and early sixties. Others may have more recently seen programs for microcomputers mainly intended for mundane and routine tasks with individual children. Fortunately, such use of the micro is not only less common in this country than in other parts of the world but is being actively rejected by educationalists in favour of more exciting possibilities.

Does the micro inhibit discussion?
Let's join a class of eleven-year-olds. They are seated informally around the micro. It is communicating with them through a 26in television screen but their eyes are by no means vacant or glazed — in fact they are not on the screen at all. Glued intently to large pictures of a pirate ship on their knees (see Figure 1) the children are searching for a hidden treasure map.

Computer
You are in the cook's store in the orlop. Call yourself a pirate! You won't find the map here. Where are you going now?

Pupils [Laughter]

Teacher
Any ideas?

PJ
I think we should change deck.

PS
It's very cold that, isn't it.

Teacher
Yes, A?

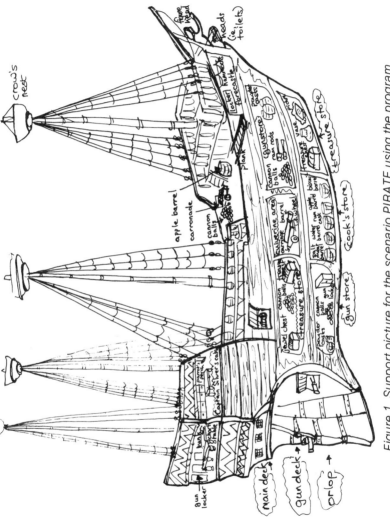

Figure 1. Support picture for the scenario PIRATE using the program SLYFOX (ITMA 'Micros in the Primary Curriculum', Module 5)

PA
Can we try the main deck?

Teacher
Is that a good idea?

Pupils
Yes, yes.

Teacher
Any reasons? T?

PT
We've got cold clues on the others — it must be the main deck.

Teacher
All right [types in].

Computer
You're on the main deck. Where now?

PT
I fancy on deck — in the crow's nest.

PM
No, Captain Silver's Cabin. He's hidden it in his own things.

Pupils
Yes, yes.

Teacher
What do you think, P?

PP
I bet he's hidden it in his cabin.

Teacher
All right [types in].

Computer
You're in Captain Silver's Cabin on the main deck. You're going to be rich! Where are you going now?

BJ
The chart table — you'd never find a map in all the charts!

PS
No, the bunk — under his pillow!

Teacher
What shall we do, M?

PM
The chart table.

Teacher
[Types in and reads] You're by the bunk in Captain Silver's Cabin on the main deck. You are warm. Where are you going now?

PS
I told you it was the bunk.

Teacher
You haven't had a turn, B . . . Any ideas?

PB
Oh — the parrot's perch.

Teacher
[types in]

PS
You'll never find it there!

Computer
You are by the parrot's perch, in Captain Silver's Cabin on the main deck. You are hot. Where now?

Teacher
Well done! Better finish it, B. Where now?

PB
Beside?

Teacher
[types in]

Computer
You've found the map!

The scene is interesting — not only because it involves a whole class but because of the amount of discussion and thought being generated. Most teachers are aware that real thinking may be more readily provoked in their pupils when they, like SLYFOX, pose genuine problems to a class rather than questions with a predictable answer — the open-ended rather than closed approach. It is, after all, the way industry and commerce stimulates problem-solving activities and 'creative' or 'productive' thought. Nevertheless, the demands such an approach has both on the personal insecurity and discipline skills of teachers tends to restrict its use to only the talented or reckless members of the profession. The others, safe in their restricted questions with predictable answers, keep discussion to a minimum, unappreciative of the occasional anecdote or opinion which may arise.

When problems such as the finding of a lost map are posed by a microcomputer the situation often changes — particularly for the teacher. Rather than feeling threatened, he or she joins the children as a participant, an observer or both — searching with the children; encouraging creative thought; humans versus machine. The disappointment of an unproductive search is soon forgotten as clues promote further investigation. Furthermore, as the structure of a program is realized through experience and rules are developed, pupils and teachers have the satisfaction of developing the most efficient strategies for their solutions to problems posed.

Rather than inhibiting oral language, therefore, the use of a microcomputer can encourage it — and not only in class lessons. Group discussions have long been recognized as an important strategy in teaching. Not only do they provide rather longer than the 20 seconds of speaking time available to pupils in the average lesson (Department of Education and Science, 1975, par 10.4) but act as '. . . a promising tool for investigating those hidden processes of our own and other people's thinking which so powerfully govern our behaviour, and about which we know so little' (Abercrombie, 1960, p 82).

The essential difference between class and group discussions is that in the latter children talk to *each other.* Pupils may well be encouraged to ask questions and seek answers in class lessons, but the main interchange of ideas is polarized towards the teacher (Figure 2a). Notice, in contrast, the network of reactions that evolves as pupils are allowed freely to talk to each other (Figure 2b).

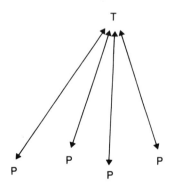 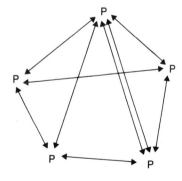

(a) The interchange of ideas in class discussions

(b) The pattern of interchange in group discussions

Figure 2 (after Abercrombie op cit *p 68)*

Such discussion, however, must have a purpose. Allowing children to chat informally about whatever interests them may have a place in school but will not necessarily promote the use of language as a tool for learning. It is in both creating opportunities for and adding purpose to informal group discussion that the microcomputer can play a part.

Four children (9 +) are using the SEEK program (see Jon Coupland's article for a more detailed description) to teach the computer differences between some selected samples of choice. The labelled products are in front of them and there is much tasting, grimacing and discussion.

P1
I think we should start with the Smoked Gruyère first, it's softer and paler than the others.

P2
But this [Leicester] is also different — it's bright orange, isn't it.

P3
Hey, look at this — doesn't it crumble [Cheshire]!

P1
My mum always buys Cheddar — look, you can cut it for toast and it grates.

P4
Ugh!

P1
What's up with you?

P4
Ugh — it's that! [Danish Blue] I'll have to go and get a drink!

P2
I told you it was strong. We have it at home.

P4
It's mouldy!

P2
No, it's not, it's good for you. You get it [blue veining] in other cheeses too like Stilton.

P3
Well, what shall we start with?

P2
Let's take Leicester and Smoked Gruyère [types them in].

Computer
A question to give the difference?

P2
What shall we say?

P1
Is it soft and light-coloured? [Yes for Smoked Gruyère].

P2
Is it orange? [Yes for Leicester].

P4
That's carrot-coloured — is it carrot-coloured? [Yes for Leicester].

P3
[Tasting] Does it taste like 'smoky bacon' crisps?

P1
No — it's my turn — I'm going to have 'Is it soft and light coloured?' [types in] . . . Yes for Smoked Gruyère, No for Leicester. OK?

P2
OK — now my turn.

The final result of the sorting exercise is shown below.

Question	Yes	No
1. Is it soft and lightly coloured?	Smoked Gruyère	2
2. Is it carrot-coloured?	Leicester	3
3. Is it strong and tangy and does it have a green mould?	Danish Blue	4
4. Is it dark yellow and rich?	Double Gloucester	5
5. Is it crumbly?	Cheshire	Cheddar

Figure 3. Sorting of cheeses with SEEK

Another group sorted the cheeses quite differently — see Figure 4 overleaf.

Question	Yes	No
1. Would you have it on toast?	2	5
2. Is it pale and mild tasting?	Cheshire	3
3. Is it orange and smooth tasting?	Leicester	4
4. Is it the only cheese sold at the corner shop?	Cheddar	Double Gloucester
5. Is it pale creamy and smoky when you taste it?	Smoked Gruyère	Danish Blue

Figure 4. Sorting of cheeses by a second group of children

The teacher carrying out this work uses SEEK as part of all his class project work. In his own words, he likes it '... because of the language it generates. Lots of my children have fathers who've been to the Falklands. We were sorting out different kinds of uniform, different kinds of ships, etc — and the arguments it caused! Do you know the difference between a frigate and a destroyer? We had to go to the library to sort that one out. Yes — I like the discussion and language we get from SEEK!'

Computers therefore can support teachers in the organization of oral tasks and promote a range of language uses in children. Such findings are not just the tentative opinions of enthusiastic observers in the field but 'hard' knowledge. In America Sheingold *et al* (1982) has shown that even in informal 'classrooms' children talk more about their work and collaborate to a greater degree when using computers than when carrying out other classroom tasks. Here in England work with the microcomputer caused more discussion and argument, less 'messing about' but more signs of enjoyment than similar activities on workcards (Stewart, 1981, p176). Observations by the ITMA team using SCAN (Systematic Classroom Analysis Notation) have also shown teachers to be more willing to alter their approach or teaching style when using the micro. Thus the computer has great potential for oral aspects of the language curriculum for teachers and pupils alike.

Does the micro inhibit writing skills?
Having considered the opportunities for children to edit creative writing by using the microcomputer as a wordprocessor (an activity far closer to the real task of writing than the spontaneous,

uncorrected items so often generated in school) readers may well be interested in how the machine may further support writing skills in school. The answer that it could replace them, therefore, may well be horrifying — but is possible! Look again at Figures 3 and 4. These are copies of actual printouts from the computer — written records of the children's work at the press of key! The real purpose of this facility is described under 'reading development', but many teachers use it, one copy per child, actually to remove the necessity for recording. This is particularly common when using SEEK with young or less able children. One teacher justifies her actions as follows.

'We are always being told to do discussion work and "thinking" exercises, but the trouble is that we have nothing to show for it in the end. Here we can set the children arguing and discussing differences. They get such a lot of good language practice and when they have finished I have something to show the headmaster and the parents. The children too get a change from "having to write about it!" This is particularly good for the slow children. They can do the thinking without being inhibited by worries over writing, spelling — the things they find difficult!'

SEEK, however, can also promote writing. Teachers have often noted how the standard of project written work improves after 'sorting' with SEEK — an obvious spin-off as children tend to research in detail differences between the items they are sorting with the program. Thus, they not only know more facts to add to their projects; they read and research!

SEEK, however, can also promote creative writing. Quite recently we have developed files for the program which create an imaginative environment which the children can explore and control until a final writing task is reached. The yes/no structure of the binary tree is still there but the atmosphere and nature of the task is very different. Here is one of *nine* routes that a child might take. Remember that the 'adventure' is only revealed to the child one stage at a time and on no occasion is the full tree visible. The child can even change its mind and come down another branch (ie, create a different story) if it wishes.

Computer
You enter a room full of strange bottles and boxes on shelves. Are you going to take one?

Child
Yes.

Computer
Open it carefully. Is there anything inside?

Child
Yes.

Computer
Are you going to eat it?

Child
No.

Computer
How sensible. Put the bottle or box down and walk to the large wardrobe in the corner of the room. Open the door. Are you going to go inside?

Child
Yes.

Computer
To your surprise you are not in a wardrobe at all. Where are you and what is happening?

Extracts from two responses, by Penny aged nine and Sarah, eleven, to this route are shown in Figures 5 and 6. Other routes generated reports for newspapers, treasure hunts, descriptions of spells, and many more. Further files for SEEK exploring the possibility of self-questioning (eg, 'If you listed your good qualities would it be longer than your list of bad qualities?') are being considered for health education. A typical writing task here might be: 'You sound quite a nice person. Draw a "happy" picture of yourself and list underneath some of the things that make you feel like that. Do the same with a "sad" picture'. Further files are based on the child viewing any scene in a book or magazine. These demand recording during several stages of the task rather than at the end and mainly exploit exploration through the senses. Finally, we are considering the complete removal of the yes/no routes in a version of SEEK so that chains of thoughts and ideas may be explored in a more open way to promote a range of creative tasks. At present, however, this is only a twinkle in the developer's eye!

   To confine any article on the potential of the micro to just writing in English lessons would, of course be ignoring the wide range of activities it can generate across the curriculum — a concern so dear to the hearts of language specialists. Below (Figure 7) is a screen print of EUREKA, a program in which children can investigate the different levels of water during typical bath-time events — putting plugs in or pulling them out of baths, turning taps on and off, climbing in and out of the water — and even singing!

In the wardrobe

In the wardrobe it smelt of
mothballs. Suddenly I felt as
if I was shrinking. I was! When
I stopped shrinking I was the
same size as a moth! I
decided to go for a walk. Then
I saw a town. It's name was
Mothia. I quickly decided that the
moth balls were not working
because there was at least
twenty moths in each house!
Then I heard a large buzz.
I looked around me and then
I saw what was making it.
The airport! I was just in
time to see a whole squadron
of moths leaving the airport
to attack a dressing gown.

Sarah McCafferty   24th November.

The Planet of Goog.

It had all started with having to deliver a shawl to old
Mrs Pears. She had asked me in and while making some
drinks she had asked me to put her shawl in the wardrobe
for her. To my surprise Mrs Pears's bedroom had shelves
all round the walls containing strange looking bottles. I had

Googlite

opened one and had hastily put back the lid when I saw
what was inside! I had then unlocked her wardrobe and
stepped inside it and to my amazement I was not in a
wardrobe anymore. So now here I was, I couldn't believe
my eyes, before me was a vast stretch of yellow, bumpy
ground. Where was I? What had happened? I decided to
explore and set off looking around me as I went. There was
no sign of life anywhere. I came to a blue bubbling swamp
and stepped back hurriedly as a fountain of green liquid
shot up and drenched me. After walking for a while I saw
in the distance a group of small bubble like houses. Just as
I was nearing them I heard a loud whoosh! and something

small whizzed past me. "Uba! Uba!" I heard from behind
me, I turned and was immediately pushed to the ground
by a strange green and red creature.

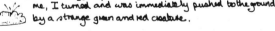

*Figures 5 and 6. Extracts from two children's ideas after an
adventure with the SEEK 'STORY' file. 'STORY' is intended to
supplement rather than replace the excellent approaches teachers
already adopt for such activities. Its unique contribution is that it
creates an environment for children to explore, their own decisions
governing the final outcome.*

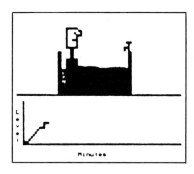

Figure 7. The story (ie, graph) and picture of one person's bath using EUREKA

After playing with the program Suzanne created her own version of events (Figure 8). After folding the paper above the graph it was given to Jonathan to interpret. Suzanne's final comments on his version of the 'story line' are found at the bottom and are very perceptive. Both children were ten years of age but had, as you can see, different personalities and abilities.

Thus the micro can aid or stimulate recording and writing in many subjects — but what about reading?

Does the micro inhibit reading development?

We have already noted the necessity created by SEEK for children to both research in books, read and follow instructions. The print-out facilities of the program were also included to teach children how to read a specialized tool — the identification key (a task that is not easy under normal circumstances). As seen in Figures 3 and 4, the printer is used to present the children's own ideas for sorting objects in a key form. By pressing certain keys a 'coded' version of the key can also be produced. Figure 9 shows the 'coded key' of some children's work with colours. Can you read it and does it work? The answers to the code are below the key.

What, however, can the micro contribute to more familiar reading tasks? For early readers and remedial children a wide range of prereading skills including visual memory, visual discrimination, sequencing and laterality can be tested or practised with the micro. Also many areas of phonic training can similarly be supported.

For teachers adopting a more holistic approach to the task, however, programs such as CLUES have as their main purpose the promotion of thinking as an essential part of the reading process. CLUES enables teachers to place in their own texts and then alter

70

STORY I thought I would have a bath so I ran the water. I let it run until it was half full with hot water no cold. I jumped in, and at once jumped out. I was to hot, so I let the water run out until it was a quater full and filled the quater I had let out with cold water then I got in and had my

PICTURES

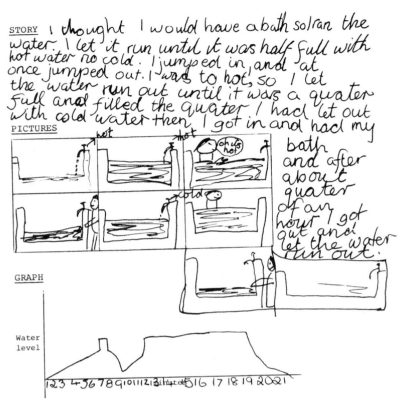

bath and after about quater of an hour I got out and let the water run out.

GRAPH

Water level

Jonathan story of my graph Puts the plug in, turns water on, rises and then gets in stays for a little while and then gets out, and it goes down, and gets in again, then it rises, and then stays in for a long time and pulls the plug out.

My comments This was quite good but Jonathan said that the first time I stayed in for a little while but I was meant the to have jumped striaght out again but my graph may have deaived him.

Figure 8. Suzanne's story using EUREKA tested on Jonathan whose version is finally marked by Suzanne. Notice the final comment.

them in some way. An obvious alteration would be the deletion of individual words for a classic Cloze procedure.

Here is the traditional 'every tenth word' deletion for a readability test. (Note that the print is much larger on the screen. For those interested, the extract is from 'Mermaid of Emmeloord' in the Hamish Hamilton *Book of Sea Legends*.)

'1. When she woke up again the lantern shone no _____. The cabin was light: the curious blue-green light _____ knew so well from her dream. The first thing _____ saw gave her a shiver of terror: her hair _____ to be standing on end, it rose right to _____ ceiling and moved softly, waving about. She was so _____ that it felt as if her body wasn't there _____ longer; when she swung the blanket aside it was _____ lighter than it had been the night before.
But _____ didn't notice this for when she swung the blanket _____ she saw a sight that nearly made her heart _____. The lower part of her body had changed into _____ glistening fishtail.'

The same text with certain verbs removed offers a quite different creative task for a group to try.

'2. When she _____ up again the lantern _____ no more. The cabin _____ light: the curious blue-green light she _____ so well from her dream. The first thing she _____ _____ her a shiver of terror: her hair _____ to be standing on end, it _____ right to the ceiling and _____ softly, waving about. She _____ so cold that it _____ as if her body _____ there any longer; when she _____ the blanket aside it _____ much lighter than it _____ _____ the night before.
But she _____ notice this for when she _____ the blanket aside she _____ a sight that nearly _____ her heart stop. The lower part of her body had _____ into a glistening fishtail.'

The scrambling of individual letters of certain words creates a very different activity.

'3. When she woke up again the <u>natnelr</u> shone no more. The <u>binac</u> was light: the curious blue-green <u>tlhgi</u> she knew so well from her <u>marde</u>. The first thing she saw gave her a shiver of <u>rertor</u>: her <u>riah</u> seemed to be standing on end, it rose right to the <u>gicenli</u> and moved softly, waving about. She was so cold that <u>ti</u> felt as if her <u>doyb</u> wasn't there any longer; when <u>hes</u> swung the <u>tlabnek</u> aside it was much lighter than it had been the <u>githn</u> before.
But <u>ehs</u> didn't notice this for when she swung the <u>ketbanl</u> aside she saw a sight that nearly made her <u>treha</u> stop. The lower part of her <u>ybdo</u> had changed into a glistening <u>ilfhsati</u>.'

72

Current key
This coded key contains the following:
Black
Silver
Blue
Gold
Light green
Dark greeny brown
Yellow
Purple
Red
Pink

Question	Yes	No
1. Is it a dark colour?	2	5
2. Can you mix colours to make it?	4	3
3. Is it the colour of blood?	A	B
4. Is it the colour of the sky?	C	9
5. Is it the colour of a face?	D	6
6. Is it expensive?	7	8
7. Is it worth about 60 pounds an ounce?	E	F
8. If you mix it with red does it make orange?	G	H
9. Does yellow and blue make it?	I	J

The code
A Red
B Black
C Blue
D Pink
E Silver
F Gold
G Yellow
H Light green
I Purple
J Dark greeny yellow

Figure 9. The 'coded key' of some children's work with colours. Try to read it and break the code! Such activities would aid the reading of a specialized format — a key — and lead to the writing, perhaps, of such tools for themselves without the micro. The 'code' is at the bottom.

Phrases too can be simply highlighted in colour. Using the printer the children can be given copies of the text and asked to underline sections that fulfil certain purposes, eg 'Underline in red sections that would help you draw a picture of the scene described in the passage. Then underline in blue words or phrases that make you think of the sea.' These can be highlighted in the computer display for checking by the children. Finally, alterations are being carried out on CLUES, to enable its use for sequencing skills — from the jumbling of words within a sentence through the jumbling of whole sentences to the rearranging of paragraphs or verses of a poem.

Conclusion
The uses of the microcomputer for language work in schools are just beginning to be explored. This article has simply contained some observations and comments on its apparent potential using a small selection of ITMA (Investigations on Teaching with Microcomputers as an Aid) programs. The computer will never replace the good teacher — and indeed may well require one for proper use. One characteristic the micro has in common with a television is a dependency on the quality of the programs for claims about its value for education. With television teachers often have to 'take what's available' and they can always just refuse to switch on. Computer users too should be similarly selective about the materials they explore with classes. Used well the micro could provide a powerful tool for the development of language skills. In the wrong hands or with the wrong programs — could it inhibit such development?

References
ABERCROMBIE, M L J, *The Anatomy of Judgement*, Hutchinson, London, 1960

BEEBY, T et al, *Systematic Classroom Analysis Notation*, Shell Centre, Nottingham University, 1979

Department of Education and Science, *A Language for Life* (The Bullock Report), HMSO, London, 1975

SHEINGOLD, K et al, *Microcomputers in School: impact on the social life of elementary classrooms*, Centre for Children and Technology, Bank Street College of Education, New York, 1982

STEWART, J G, *The Potential of the Microcomputer in Aiding the Teaching of Primary Science*, unpublished MPhil thesis, Nottingham University, 1981

Programs
All the programs described are published through Longman by ITMA/Shell Centre, College of St Mark and St John, Derriford Road, Plymouth, PL6 8BH.

Using a database

Patrick Scott, Head of English, Pendleton Sixth Form College, Salford

One way of establishing how pupils preparing for public exams are taught to read is to have a look at what they are given to read. And one way of speculating about what they are given to read is to look at the exam papers they will eventually be sitting. Considering the number of exam boards, there is a surprising degree of uniformity about these exam papers. It would be almost impossible to distinguish between one board and another merely by looking at the style of their 'comprehension' tests. The chances are, for example, that most of the passages selected will be taken either from novels or from a certain kind of stylish non-fiction. They are likely to have been written in continuous prose organized in paragraphs and they will almost all be constructed in the assumption that the reader will start at the beginning and read in an orderly manner to the end. It seems a reasonable supposition that that represents the kind of reading diet that we give our pupils and there are all kinds of admirable reasons why this should be so. By and large, novels are likely to provide the most interesting kind of material available, they offer examples of excellence in using the written word, and they provide plenty of opportunity for follow-up work that is undeniably worthwhile.

If, however, you stop and think for a moment about the kind of reading that most pupils are likely to do after they leave school or college, you may start to feel a little uneasy. For most, the bulk of their reading will be either more functional or more casual — newspapers, for example, recipes or tax forms. Yet if the evidence of exam papers is anything to go by, we simply assume that reading skills are transferable and let our pupils get on with it. It's a big assumption to make if you consider how you actually read a newspaper, a recipe or a tax form. Unless you are exceptionally methodical, you are unlikely to start at the beginning and read through to the end. What you will probably do is skim the entire document in a more or less desultory fashion depending on whether you are reading for entertainment or profit. You may read more closely anything that catches the eye, or demands closer attention for one reason or another, but even then you are unlikely to read it in the way you would read a novel. Each type of reading material demands a different reading strategy.

The most obvious reason why English teachers do not turn eagerly to this kind of material is probably the most accurate one —

pupils may find it boring. It's hard to compete with the likes of Billy Caspar and Billy Liar. The recognition of difficulties, however, should not be an excuse for ducking out of them, and so I decided to try and find some way of solving the problem.

A great deal of the work I do in an open-access urban sixth form college is with students 'repeating' English language courses in one year — the target group for the proposed 17 + exam. Most of the curriculum development work that has been undertaken in this area has been rather haphazard and uncoordinated. None the less, there is some agreement that work should be in the broadest sense vocational and that 'English' or 'communication' should equip students with practical skills. My sympathy with this point of view seemed to put the curriculum ball firmly in my court. My conviction that students should be able to read information that comes to them in a variety of forms — lists, printouts, official forms, graphic displays and so on was the starting point. The problem with this kind of material, however, is that it is usually only read under very special circumstances. Train timetables are consulted in order to catch trains. The motivation is all-important. Some of the exam papers in 'communication' that reprint timetables and expect students to imagine that they have a train to catch seem to forget this. I felt that if students were to approach this kind of work with any kind of enthusiasm, the material would have to be rather more closely related to their actual circumstances than it sometimes is. This requirement posed new problems since it made it even more difficult to see where I was going to find appropriate material.

The use of a simple database suggested itself as a solution for a number of different reasons. I had better explain, before going any further, what I mean by a 'simple database' as I have some hopes that this may be read by somebody who has little knowledge of computers and only a passing interest in them. One of the most valuable features of a computer is its capacity to store information, and search through it more rapidly than can be done by conventional means. At its most sophisticated, this is why, for example, the police keep information on computer files. When, as in school, you are working with a micro, it is quite possible to use the machine in a similar way, though of course on a much smaller scale. An example may help to illustrate what this means in practice. Imagine that a class were studying the behaviour of birds in a certain geographical area. The data they collected about, for example, frequency of sightings, time of day and so on could be put into a computer which would then be able to process it in potentially useful ways. It could easily provide information about, say, which type of bird was most likely to be seen at a particular time of day, and even a fairly small computer could handle more information of this kind than it would be convenient to deal with in any other way.

I felt that there was some potential here for an exercise to introduce my students to new 'reading' skills, as their involvement in compiling the information would give them a vested interest in making sense of it. It might provide a way of overcoming the drawbacks of those worthy but unattractive 'communication' syllabuses.

The subject matter of the survey, however, had to be right. Given the ability level and commitment of these students, I had to be careful to ensure that the information was fairly freely available and that it would not present too many problems when being fashioned into the standardized format that the computer would require. Eventually, I settled on a survey of part-time work for students in Salford. Over half the group of 20 had part-time jobs, and friends with similar experience could easily be found. Students of this age, moreover, evince the same kind of interest as adults in discovering whether they earn more or less that the person sitting next to them.

I predetermined all but one of the headings under which information would be gathered. I would have preferred to have allowed the students to define all the categories themselves, but it would have required more sophisticated programming, and I had had to write the program myself as a commercial program was not available. A series of questions were flashed up on the screen and answered by typing information in through the keyboard. After the data had been entered, the screen looked something like this:

PART-TIME WORK — SALFORD

EMPLOYER? TESCO
TYPE OF WORK? ASSISTANT
TOTAL HOURS? 12
TOTAL BREAKS? 2
PAY? 15
AGE? 16
SEX? FEMALE
REGULATIONS? UNIFORM
DO YOU WISH TO CREATE
ANOTHER CATEGORY (Y/N)?

The final question was asked only once. If the answer was 'no', then it never reappeared, if 'yes', the computer added another question to the list already provided. In my explanation to the group I had created a heading 'rating' and given each job a star value from 1 to 5, like hotels in the AA guide. I pointed out to them that they were not bound by this and the ensuing discussion was almost as valuable as if they had determined all the categories themselves. Eventually, they plumped for 'district', an important consideration for them, but one which I had overlooked because, being a driver, I was far more mobile than they were. The discussion illustrated very vividly what a category is and how information can be arranged. The importance of this will not be underestimated by anybody who has confronted the problem of teaching students to argue effectively on paper.

The students gathered information and typed it into the computer. Most of the class were content to watch the information being typed in and to contribute their own when the time came. One small group, however, were becoming restless and, in order to give them something to do, I asked them to decide what questions it would be useful to ask, once the database had been created. Their first attempts revealed how slender was their grasp of how computers worked. Because they had a sense of computers as something magical, they failed to recognize the relationship between the answers they might be given and the information that had been put in. They suggested, for example, that we should try to get a comparative printout of rates of pay in department stores and other kinds of shops. Once they had grasped that this couldn't be done because no such category existed, they began to formulate more useful suggestions. What they finally requested was that the information be printed out in a number of different ways:

(a) by district, distinguishing between jobs in Manchester and those outside

(b) by sex

(c) by age, distinguishing between 16-, 17- and 18-year-olds

(d) all jobs paying £9.00 or more regardless of hours worked.

I had anticipated (b) above, and had also made provision for lists to be printed out according to 'type' of job. I had not foreseen their other suggestions, and was forced to spend some time re-programming the computer. That was not quite as formidable as it sounds, but I can see no reason why a commercial program suitable for work of this kind shouldn't make it fairly easy for the operator to select various different ways of printing out information.

The students were then given three A4 sheets of printouts. The following is merely a selection.

FULL LIST (Extract)

WOOLWORTH	ASSISTANT	RATE: £1.14	MANCHESTER
CURTESS	ASSISTANT	RATE: £1.12	SALFORD
TESCO	CASHIER	RATE: £1.00	SALFORD
MARKET	ASSISTANT	RATE: £1.00	MANCHESTER
PRIVATE	SELLING	RATE: £0.50	LIVERPOOL
NEWANS	ASSISTANT	RATE: £1.00	SALFORD
DAIRY	ASSISTANT	RATE: £1.28	FARNWORTH

LIST BY SEX (Extract)

FEMALE

TOP SHOP	CLEANER
LEWIS'S	ASSISTANT
GREGG'S	ASSISTANT
MARKET	ASSISTANT
PRIVATE	BABY SITTING
MARKET HALL	ASSISTANT

MALE

PRIVATE	SELLING
VIRGIN RECORDS	SELLING

LIST BY DISTRICT (Extract)

OUTSIDE MANCHESTER

SUPADRUG	CASHIER	RATE:	£1.21
CHIP SHOP	ASSISTANT	RATE:	£2.00
SPORTS SHOP	ASSISTANT	RATE:	£0.94

MANCHESTER

LEWIS'S	ASSISTANT	RATE:	£1.43
WOOLWORTH'S	ASSISTANT	RATE:	£1.14
NEWSAGENT	ASSISTANT	RATE:	£1.00

My eventual aim was that the students should use the information to write a guide to part-time work. My immediate task was to ensure that they could find their way around the printouts I had given them. I devised a set of questions to be used as the basis for discussion. The initial questions were merely factual — 'Which is the best-paid job?', for example. Later questions were more sophisticated, requiring two or more printouts to be compared with each other —

'Are boys better paid than girls?'. Finally, I included one or two questions that demanded that students bring their own judgement and experience into play — 'Is it easier for girls to get jobs than boys?' and 'Why do rates of pay vary?'. I hoped that this would demonstrate both the value and the limitations of the exercise, that information can be sorted in a variety of different ways, but that the need for interpretation remains.

Some of these hopes were fulfilled, though I was disappointed by the way in which perceptive comments about the issues were sometimes met with scepticism about the reliability of the survey, rather than counter argument. I was quite prepared to accept that the scepticism was justified, but where I could see the value of suspending disbelief, the students could not. None the less, some interesting discussion ensued, particularly about the quite subtle sex distinctions between jobs that the survey revealed.

The final stage of the exercise was the writing up of the survey. In preparing the students for this, I became so preoccupied with the problems they might encounter in trying to reduce this mass of information to manageable proportions, that I failed to recognize the difficulties they would encounter merely by being asked to write a report. As a consequence I devoted most of the time available to us to a discussion of different ways of presenting data. The students used the blackboard to draw bar graphs and pie charts, and we talked about the advantages and disadvantages of visual and verbal presentation. They agreed that writing was useful when you weren't sure about something, or when things 'needed explaining'. Graphs and charts, on the other hand, were considered to be more valuable as a way of presenting figures and statistics clearly. What I failed to do was to spend time asking them what they as potential readers as well as writers would actually want from a guide of the kind that I envisaged. Neither did I spend enough time looking at how professionals compile reports like this, or giving them some idea of the kind of sections into which it might be divided. This was a serious omission, which I intend to put right next year. It meant that the work I received was full of excellent and ingenious graphic displays of the information, but short on analysis and a sense of audience. I could feel confident that the students had discovered how to read the data very efficiently, but not that they had learned to use it in a practical context.

Nevertheless, there were some achievements. Here is Tracy looking for an explanation for the fact that 'the type of jobs done by females compared with the type of jobs done by males is exceptionally different'. She suggests that 'males tend to think all shop work is done by females, but to me, I think that it should be done by both . . . looking at the results obtained the males tend to go for record shops and sport shops. This may be because they think that Woolworth's, Curtess and Wimpey foods, for example, are just for girls to work in'. She also goes to some trouble to analyse the types of shops that offer work and produces an elaborate pie chart showing the results:

Her explanation of the small number of students finding work in supermarkets is that 'they [the supermarket managers] can get government training and why should they pay out when they can get work done and pay nothing out'.

Mike attaches to a bar graph the following comment: 'There are more female than male because our survey could mostly only get girls to say their jobs, and also most factories are closing down where a boy is more likely to find a job'.

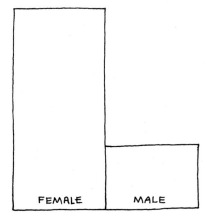

Phil, ambitiously, offers an explanation of the whole phenomenon of part-time work: 'One could say that it is a good deal easier to obtain part-time employment than full-time employment. Maybe it's because of the depression causing a massive comeback in market trading.'

If there was a lesson to be learned from these successes, it was that students needed to be taught to look not for solutions but for problems. Both Tracy and Mike seemed, in their visual displays, to have highlighted anomalies in a way that made it difficult to resist looking for explanations.

Finally, and less obviously, there were some students who managed to give purpose to their observations by the way in which they presented them. Julie gives sound advice — 'this pie chart shows that if you want a part-time job, the best place to look is in the larger stores because they always seem to be taking on more staff'. Phil, however, goes one better. His direct, colloquial style is quite deliberate, and seems to me a wholly appropriate way of addressing students looking for work: 'It would be almost impossible to put your finger on the perfect job although private shops seem to be on the lookout for no messing, cheap labour. Hence market halls, sports, Newmans, newsagents and greengrocers are all paying at a rate of £1.00 or under.'

English teaching and computer-assisted simulations

Chris Harrison, Head of Central Information Unit, English Language and Literature Division, The British Council

What are you teaching your students and why? These are the two burning questions that have to be answered before we can begin to look at the position of computers in the classroom. Fine — I am teaching them English. What kind? English literature (Scots, Welsh, Irish, Australian, literature in English)? English grammar? Writing skills in English? Listening skills? Speaking or reading skills? A mixture of all of these? Then what is the relationship between the studying of Nigerian plays and appropriately completing a job application form? Strange, isn't it, that facility and competence in any one of these areas often points to ability in the others? And where do computers fit in? First things first!

Why, then, do we promote learning in these subject areas of English language and literature in English? In the final analysis of the 'why?', we as English teachers are engaged in promoting language as communication, as a communicative activity as much as a part of our cultural background. We seek to promote the effective transfer of ideas and instructions, to ensure that the student learns to manipulate language in order to attract and hold attention, to cajole, to express dislike or preference in a wide variety of real situations. Language is a tool which can only be exploited to its fullest if students are given intensive training and practice in as many of its known uses as possible. We should investigate any method or aid that will help them to use language meaningfully and communicatively. Certainly it seems that computers have plenty to offer in this area.

In recent years there has been much research done in the field of needs analysis, and in ensuring that what is learned in the classroom is fitting and appropriate for the students' future needs (see especially Munby, 1978). While accepting that, without doubt, such analyses are an essential part of answering the 'Why?' question, 'this overriding preoccupation with target discourse and behaviours, diverts attention from the immediate situation in which both learners and teachers find themselves' (Patrick Early in British Council, 1982). What we do in the classroom, then, is as 'real' as what we do outside it. How we communicate in the learning situation, between teachers and students as much as between students themselves, is as valid as outside it — or beyond it.

It is only in the past ten years or so that the learning of language has begun to take place in the student-centred classroom instead of the teacher/textbook dominated arena. However, it is only in the last two years or so that teachers have themselves been able to show that virtually all computer software available has reflected the older methodologies in which empty vessels were slowly filled through patience, an occasional shake-up, and other well known techniques. How narrow some of those vessels' necks were too! The result is that although there are many textbooks and other aids available (I would often include the teacher as an aid) to promote student-centred activity, there is virtually no computer software commercially available that allows for this. Before the personal micro's arrival, programmers appear to have taken no notice of research into the actual learning process.

I believe that one of the most important aspects of the classroom is feedback. The teacher constantly monitors for confirmation of learning and the teacher frequently gives the learner progress reports — written, spoken and signalled. This basic practice has hardly changed since Plato wrote 'The Ion' in the fourth century BC! There is a steady progression from the known to the unknown, with students expecting the teacher to ask them questions about what they know already, and for the teacher to act as 'knower' and informant. The process resembles an ongoing quiz. As results come in they are analysed by the teacher, and appropriate feedback received by both teacher and learner. Progression is controlled by the teacher, or, as it may be, by the computer. And, indeed, if this sums up what goes on in some classrooms, then the teacher's role may well become no more than that of a technician!

The danger to the profession occurs, I think, when the role of the teacher is seen as quiz-master rather than as learning-promoter, for the untiring computer excels at this. On its own, however, the computer can be no better than the remote (in time and place) program designer. The 'encyclopaedia' on which the 'quiz' is based remains relatively static compared to the rate with which the learner learns, and the computer can draw only on the information it contains, not on the knowledge it has amassed and certainly not on an understanding of the subject that the teacher laboriously achieves.

When we look at the various roles that computers are being used to carry out in today's classroom, we can discern the following.

— Paper analogues in which text (or text and graphics) is shown on the screen either for simple reading tasks or for reading comprehension.

— Quiz-masters which present (usually) pre-set quizzes either of the multiple-choice kind or of the essay question type. The former can be scored automatically, while the latter (unless the required answer is specific) needs an interpreted score by the teacher. Such programs can also be used by teachers alone as a simple kind of wordprocessor in the preparation of tests.

— Stimulators of deductive reasoning. Examples of this kind are Tim Johns' (for the 16K Sinclair) and my own (for TRS-80) PLURALS where the student's task is to find out what the computer does not know, thereby insisting on some form of real interaction.

— Framework for student or teacher to work in. Chris Jones' CROSSWORD program, as well as most wordprocessing packages and several author languages, provides these frameworks.

— Any of the above dressed up as a game — such as my own NOUGHTS AND CROSSES and SNAKES AND LADDERS, in which a game ostensibly is played, but where success in the game has to be followed by success in a quiz. The advantage of this kind of role for the computer is that it is ideally suited for students working in pairs or teams either competitively or in cooperation.

— Simulations in which the computer takes on the role of informant for a group of students.

A simulation is defined (British Council, 1979) as 'an activity in which students discuss a problem which is in a setting that has been clearly described to them. Students apply their own knowledge and experience to this information thus giving them the basic data to discuss the problem'. It is a 'representation which employs substitute elements to replace real or hypothetical components' (B Dimitrou in Armstrong and Taylor, 1971). This kind of activity employs role simulation (where the student is himself) or role-play (where the student takes on the part of a character). There are other definitions of what a simulation is, but I shall be thinking in these terms in what follows.
    Computer simulations have been imaginatively used for many branches of learning — especially those in which real practice is dangerous, expensive or foolhardy. Examples can be drawn from aviation, medicine, architecture, and other practical fields. Few budding pilots would relish crashing a real aeroplane: none of us would volunteer to be practised on by young medical students. How many people would live in experimental buildings? Yet by using

simulated situations, settings can be created that allow experimentation and risk-taking with no physical danger, though, of course, teachers should be aware of the possible psychological dangers that might occur when normal classroom conventions and restrictions are removed. How can the English teacher now benefit from the possibilities that have already been explored in these other disciplines?

John Higgins has written (for the 16K Sinclair) a pleasant version of 'Cluedo', called MURDER, in which lower intermediate students practise past tenses. Suspects are summoned, questioned and accused by the student playing the part of the investigating police officer and using various forms of the past tense. Other settings can readily be imagined for practising particular language acts — planning for foreign travel, timetabling meetings, planning shopping expeditions, designing a structure from given parts, and so on.

I have used a variant of this in my TOWN PLANNING program which was originally devised as a management investigation tool — to simulate decision-making behaviour and to analyse if and how a leader emerges from a group. The computer program contains no actual language stimuli and holds closely to the definition of simulations as given above, and, in contrast to other simulation programs, the computer performs no analyses of the student's behaviour. In this respect it places no constraints on communicative activity, allowing real combinations of classroom talk and discourse types to emerge through the imposed roles and the setting. This program has aroused a great deal of interest both from within and outside the English teaching profession, and it is perhaps worth describing it in a little more detail.

A setting is given — a small town with high unemployment, in which a new, but potentially smelly, factory is to be sited. Conflicting roles are given to up to six students (bus driver, allotment keeper, factory owner, librarian, etc), and their task is to recommend a site for the new factory. At any time they may review their roles, to ensure that their attitudes and points of view remain consistent. In addition, they may mark on a map of the town features such as one-way streets, zebra-crossings and so on, so that they can study the effects of their decisions on traffic and pedestrian flow. As various options are proposed, players interpose their own priorities and preoccupations in appropriate ways using a very large number of rhetorical and psychological techniques. Since there can be no 'wrong' or 'right' answer the skills of diplomacy and compromise in debate are thoroughly exercised, and all the emotions of a strongly felt debate can be stirred.

Now, what part does the teacher play in this kind of activity? The machine has been switched on, and the students have identified themselves rapidly with the debating roles. But who is noting that certain ways of presenting a case are more powerful, that particular body signs strengthen or weaken an individual's communicative ability, that under stress or attack some students clarify, others lose sight of their main arguing positions? Here, then, is what I see to be the teacher's role during simulations: to watch, listen to, interpret, and perhaps summarize the communicative behaviour of the students, and to help them plan remedial or reinforcing action, to help them overcome their weaknesses and build on their strengths. This is not to say, of course, that the teacher should not participate in the simulation. Often quite the reverse — by participating, the teacher brings greater authenticity to the situation and adds greater power to the necessary follow-up. The computer acts purely as an aid to the simulation, keeping minds on a predefined setting, but not interrupting the activity, and demanding no skills (eg, typing) relating to the interfacing of human and machine.

It has not gone unnoticed by many of us that many 'adventure' games may contain useful simulation material. Discovery, exploration, strategy and corporate planning may all be useful ways of harnessing a group of students to indulge in valuable communicative activity. One game that has proved very useful in getting overseas students to practise commands and direction-giving is PYRAMID by Radio Shack. Although the linguistic interface between player and machine is limited to words like 'drop' (responds with 'drop what?') and 'East' or just plain 'E' (responds with 'There is no way that direction'), the excitement and interest that the decision-making process arouses in a small group is quite considerable. [Most of these games have two distinct limitations. One is a very limited vocabulary added to which some versions insist that all commands must be expressed in two words only. The other is despite the fact that the situational dilemma may require lateral solutions, usually only one solution to each problem is accepted. — Ed.]

With adventure games there is a real spirit of discovery and exploration. Poking around in uncharted areas, such as a maze, can produce many utterances that only the most tortuous of textbook exercises can test. 'I shouldn't go that way, if I were you', 'Wouldn't it be better if . . .', or 'We ought to have gone down instead of up . . .' will all easily and spontaneously emerge, unasked for, to be picked up easily by the less fluent speaker and used naturally thereafter.

There are plenty of adventure titles for the adventurous English teacher to choose from, suiting most makes of popular micro.

ASYLUM II — 'You begin in an institution and must successfully negotiate not just the institute itself, but four other dream adventures as well . . . concentrate, or you may never escape the nightmare of the institute!' sounds promising. DOUBLE AGENT, DRAGON QUEST, DUNGEONS AND DRAGONS, THE ARROW OF DEATH, MYSTERY FUN HOUSE, and ADVENTURE LAND, are just a very few of the titles available. In choosing between them, word of mouth and what are known as 'addictiveness ratings' are the only criteria available since few programs may be viewed or tried out before being bought. It becomes increasingly important, therefore, to join one of the many 'user groups' that exist for each machine if you are going to use adventure games as semi-simulations. For the talented, however, it is possible to buy adventure game skeleton programs, which allow you to write your own adventure. Perhaps both the designing and the use of such creations would result in useful communicative activity!

A relatively new type of computer-based simulation is only now just becoming available — interactive video. Using this technique, which is a combination of video and microcomputer, students can see actual film reflecting the results of their decisions. At the moment primarily of interest to personnel trainers in industry and commerce, the technique holds great promise for students of literature (excerpts from plays, for example) as well as adding pictorial accompaniment to role-playing and role simulations.

To return to the original questions: 'What are you teaching your students and why?', we may now add 'How?' Taking the premise that our students learn English in order to build up their communicative abilities (although the cultural element also plays a large part), we may need to place more emphasis on fluency than accuracy activities, on task-centred activities than on language-centred activities, on interaction between students rather than on one-way teacher – student traffic. We need to allow the students to take risks without being threatened by penalties, to cooperate rather than compete, to introduce the unexpected and to take the initiative. By giving the 'information role' to a computer, and by the teacher taking on the 'analyst' and 'planner' roles, we can provide for all of these needs in a student-centred setting.

References

ARMSTRONG, E H R and TAYLOR, J L, *Feedback on Institutional Simulation Systems*, Cambridge Institute of Education, 1971
BRITISH COUNCIL, *Simulations, ELT Guide 2*, NFER/Nelson, 1979
BRITISH COUNCIL, *Humanistic Approaches: an empirical view*, 1982
MUNBY, JOHN, *Communicative Syllabus Design*, Cambridge University Press, 1978

Generating alternatives

Tim Johns, English for Overseas Students Unit, University of Birmingham

In this paper I shall be describing some experimental work using the computer in the teaching of English as a foreign language, and pointing to some of the ways in which it has broken with the more traditional approach — stemming largely from the United States of America — to computer-assisted instruction in foreign languages. That tradition depended largely for its hardware on large and expensive mainframe computers linked to student terminals (visual display units and keyboards); for its motivation on the prestige and mystique associated with the equipment itself; for its software on teacher-created tests, drill-and-practice exercises and programmed learning; and for its theoretical underpinning on the behaviouristic view of language-learning as a matter of habit-information. Despite the very moderate success of such materials when used with that earlier technological marvel, the language laboratory, there are reports of good success rates and continuing student interest when computers have been used in this way. These results can hardly be attributed solely to 'computer charisma', and are likely to be connected with two factors that make arcade games so popular: the active feedback on success/failure that the machine can give, and, linked to that, the possibility of 'having another go'. Even the most tedious drill can, when presented on the computer, be used by the student as a game, and much computer-assisted learning material exploits the game element. Nevertheless, it is natural that the vision of a future in which rows of students sit tapping away at their terminals should be repugnant to a great many language teachers: it is a world away from their conviction that language should be learnt in the same way as it is used — that is to say, as a total communicative activity — and that the use of machines to drill fragmented 'language patterns' divorced from context may be of marginal benefit in that learning.

In the last two or three years the stereotype of computer-assisted learning has come under attack not only from those who would make it a reason for excluding the computer from serious consideration as a tool in language-learning, but also from some teachers who have sought to give it a more imaginative and creative role in the learning process. One of the factors underlying this change has been the 'microcomputer revolution' of the late 1970s. Computers began to appear in schools (though still in small numbers) and began to be sold as desirable consumer goods alongside hi-fi equipment and washing machines; and either at school or at home some language-teachers have begun to experiment with ways in which they could be used in their teaching. In the process the computer has lost much of the forbidding mystique that once shrouded it (it is difficult to be intimidated or impressed by a £50 ZX81, for example), and with the mystique there have also gone many of the previous preconceptions about how computers should be used. The particular preconception that I wish to focus on in this paper is that whatever the computer presents to the student must have been created in advance by the teacher and written into a teaching program, and that the role of the computer is restricted to presenting such pre-established tasks, checking input, giving feedback and keeping score. The generative approach to computer-assisted learning, by contrast, entails that no tasks are written in advance: what the computer program consists of is a series of instructions allowing the machine to create such tasks on the basis of its moment-by-moment interaction with the student. I wish, furthermore, to suggest that in giving the computer this more active role, we may also find that we can help to release the creative, investigative abilities of our students.

The generative approach to computer-assisted learning has, of course, an immediate and obvious appeal to the teacher. The writing of drills and exercises can become a chore in which imagination all too easily flags. That chore becomes even more time-consuming when any exercise has to be presented through the medium of the computer: it has been suggested that one hour of computer teaching requires 50 – 100 hours of programming time. That equation can be altered in favour to the materials-writer by the use of 'authoring languages' such as PILOT which provide a simple format for the input of questions and answers, and ready-made routines for answer-checking and so forth; but even with such assistance, the provision of an adequate supply of learning materials can be a daunting task. If, on the other hand, the machine can be programmed to generate the materials, and to do so in such a way that it creates a different exercise every time the program is used, the whole basis of the equation (the assumption of a teaching output fixed in advance and therefore measurable in terms of 'teaching time') is overturned. The argument for generative CAL however, is not solely based on teachers' natural indolence, attractive though that argument is to me as an indolent teacher. A further benefit can arise from the very nature of a computer program, which has to be completely explicit in telling the obedient but stupid machine what to do. It is, therefore an excellent test-bed for the teacher's linguistic and pedagogic insights: the job of writing a program and trying it out can lead to the realization that assumptions we make about how a language works, and how it is taught and learnt, may need to be looked at afresh. To take some examples from my own work referred to below: if I had not tried to write computer programs I would not have realized that in English 'as long as' does *not* mean 'the same length as'; nor would I have been led to investigate how the introduction of digital clocks and watches seems to be changing the way in which we tell the time; nor would I have had to consider the exact circumstances in which a student expects a teacher to be silent, or laconic, or verbose.

From the point of view of the student, there are more important advantages to the generative approach. It can give the possibility of far greater variety in that every task is a new task created on the spot for him. Moreover, it allows far greater flexibility in catering for individual needs, interests, and progress — and, because of the greater choice that flexibility implies, greater scope for the student to direct his or her own learning. In future developments we should be able to add the benefit of adaptivity: that is to say, the program will be written in such a way that it 'learns' from the way in which students interact with it, and on the basis of that learning, prepares its tasks more effectively.

In considering how the generative principle can be put into effect I wish to distinguish between two approaches, one of which may be called *analytic* and the other *synthetic*. Each approach in turn may employ two basic strategies which, for lack of better terms, I shall call *unintelligent* and *intelligent*.

The basic idea behind *unintelligent analysis* is that the computer program operates on language held in the computer or — in some programs — input by the student. That language may be at the level of word, sentence, or text. The program then performs a 'mechanical' analysis of the language in terms of the constituents of the language — that is to say, where and what the letters, word boundaries, sentence boundaries, etc, are — the nature of the analysis depending on the next step in the program. That step involves the systematic and controlled manipulation or degradation of the language in order to generate a language-learning task. Four such manipulations are possible:

— reordering
— deletion
— substitution
— insertion.

Some games using these techniques are already familiar:

HANGMAN, used in English-as-a-foreign-language classrooms throughout the world, and now available in a number of computer versions, employs deletion; while an anagram-generating program is based on the idea of reordering. Both of these games, however, operate at word level only. My own interest in computer-assisted learning arose from the idea of using such techniques on continuous text. My JUMBLER program, written in 1980 for a DEC20 mainframe, was a suite of games based on the idea of reordering. In 'Jumbleparagraph', the sentences of the text were randomly reordered, the student having to reconstitute the text in the original order. In 'Jumblechunk', the words in a section of text between punctuation marks were reordered, the student having again to restore the original order; and in 'Jumbleword' the student had to identify and reconstitute an anagrammed word in the text, using clues from the context to help find the answer. All the games had a gambling format: the student was given an initial stock of points, and for each task odds based on the difficulty of the task (the computer estimating this in terms of the number of sentences in the text, words in the chunk, or letters in the word. The student in making a wager had, in order to play the game effectively, to estimate the likelihood that he or she had found the right answer, and could bet low where it was clear that there might be some ambiguity about the ordering. Recently I have begun the task of transferring JUMBLER to a microcomputer (the Grundy Newbrain), using experience gained when students played the mainframe version. I realized, for example, that in 'Jumbleparagraph' students needed an opportunity to try out the effect of different sentence-orders on screen, and the microcomputer version provides a 'scratchpad' allowing rapid and easy manipulation of the text.

A text game using deletion is my TEXTBAG (also for the Newbrain but originally in an uncompleted mainframe version called MASKER), which is an extension to its logical limits of the Cloze principle. In a Cloze text every *n*th word is deleted from a text (the most usual interval being seven), the student having to restore the missing words. Cloze is, of course, readily implemented in a computer, the advantage of computer-generated Cloze being that the student may choose the interval with which he or she wishes to work. In contrast with the *partial* deletion of Cloze, TEXTBAG is based on the idea of *total* deletion: each letter in the text is replaced by ' ~ ', leaving only information about word divisions and punctuation. The hidden text is accompanied by a simple information question or a statement to be completed on the basis of the text.

It is the task of the student to 'uncover' as much of the text as may be necessary to answer the question, the sooner the answer is found the greater the reward that is offered. The student is able to control a cursor which may be placed under any hidden word in the text: that word may then be 'bought' from his stock of points (the gambling principle again), or, given enough context, guessed to gain points. Another program using the principle of total deletion is John Higgins' STORYBOARD: in that program the Hangman principle is applied to the text; and *all* occurrences of a correctly guessed word are inserted. In linguistic terms, TEXTBAG is based on the idea of *token* replacement and STORYBOARD on *type* replacement.

The most obvious difference between the traditional CAL drill and games such as JUMBLER, TEXTBAG and STORYBOARD is that the first is usually based on isolated sentences, while the last employs continuous (usually paragraph-length) text. There are some further differences that may be worth summarizing briefly. The drill emphasizes language as code: the text game emphasizes language as communication, and in particular the information a text conveys, and the way that information hangs together. The aim of drill is to reinforce appropriate linguistic habits: does the student respond with the correct answer? The aim of the text game is to develop the student's ability to form appropriate hypotheses and to guess intelligently: can the student discover the correct answer? The drill is essentially authoritarian, and the student's role within it passive. The text game, on the other hand, emphasizes student autonomy and student choice both within the game itself and in the situation in which it is used. To develop this last point a little further, our aim is to build up a series of games using the four principles of manipulation outlined above, and in parallel with them files of texts at different levels and in different genres and subject areas, ranging from children's stories and newspaper extracts to texts on electrical engineering or accountancy. Giving the student the opportunity to select both game and texts will allow a flexibility that would hardly be possible without the computer — a flexibility which could be of particular value where the student has a specialist purpose in learning English and it may be impossible to find, or uneconomic to prepare, man-written materials to meet that student's particular needs.

The possibility of *intelligent analysis* for language-learning is still largely to be explored. One technique which has been used is pattern-recognition. Jørgen Christiansen, for example, has been working on a spelling analyser: that is to say, a program which will not only detect that a word has been misspelt, but which is also able to classify the error involved (static or dynamic reversal, consonant doubling, etc). My programs S-ENDING and A/AN for the unexpanded ZX81 use another application of the technique. Both reverse the usual expectation that the machine should set the student tasks to solve: they adopt, instead, an 'exploratory' approach in which it is up to the students to set tasks for the machine to solve. Such programs are inappropriate for individual self-access, but can be powerful stimulators of group discussion: for example, when the computer is used as an 'intelligent blackboard' with a class. The focus of activity may be either to 'defeat' the program by thinking up tasks which it cannot solve, or to discover the principle it is applying to produce its solutions.

In A/AN the computer's offer is to place the correct form of the indefinite article before any noun phrase that the user cares to type in: on the basis of very simple pattern-recognition techniques it is able to distinguish between such difficult cases as 'an uninformed person' and 'a uniformed person', and between 'a sob' and 'an SOB'. Similar work has been done by Hanno Martin for German, although there the focus has been on syntax, using automatic parsing techniques: this is one of the many areas in which computer-assisted learning may expect to borrow in future from theoretical work in artificial intelligence.

The idea of *unintelligent synthesis* is based on the ability of the computer to take decisions randomly. Using the computer equivalent of the familiar substitution table, we can program the machine to synthesise samples of language, whether for practice, or — as with programs which offer to 'write poetry' or 'tell fortunes' — for fun. There is nothing new in our readiness to be entertained by such random processes of creation: it can be found throughout the seventeenth and eighteenth centuries, from John Peters' machine for the automatic writing of Latin hexameters, to Mozart's *Werfelspiel,* which was in effect a program (recently implemented on a microcomputer) for the random generation of minuets. It was over 250 years ago that Jonathan Swift, in *Gulliver's Travels,* satirised such endeavours, mocking the absurdity of the unintelligent machine producing language, and the absurdity of the language that the unintelligent machine can produce. The satire remains valid: nevertheless, we may for teaching purposes exploit that very adsurdity, requiring the student to reduce or to justify it. In Burkhard Leuschner's DIALOG-CRIT, for example, the computer suggests to the student that they should both try to write dialogues. The computer, however, confesses that its own efforts are not very good, as becomes apparent from the examples it begins to produce:

AT THE DOCTOR'S

A Good morning, Madam. What can I do for you?
B Hi, my lord. Mum sent me for a bowl of soap . . . etc.

Can the student improve the computer's efforts? The program asks the student to correct and edit the dialogue on screen, and then print out the revised version to show to the teacher.

We may, however, expect the machine to avoid such absurdities in advance. There are two ways in which this can be done. One is by careful preselection of the elements to be synthesised, and of the frame or frames in which they are placed. Thus was the method adopted by Peters and Mozart: and a careful teacher constructing a substitution table for classroom use will try to ensure that, while it generates a large number of examples, none of them are too wildly improbable. This requires considerable linguistic sensitivity of lexical sets, and the potential use of language. Since these are all essential elements in language learning, it is natural to consider how far it may be possible to develop such sensitivity by giving the learner an opportunity to develop or modify simple language generators. Work on these lines with poetry and story generators for first-language teaching has been reported by Papert, Chandler, Sharples and others: there is no reason why the same principle should not be applied in foreign-language teaching, although there the emphasis might be more on non-literary texts — for example, dialogues, letters, and reports.

The second way of controlling the output of a language generator is to write the program in such a way that the computer 'understands' the language it produces. Our own understanding of language rests on and mediates our overall understanding of the real world to which language refers. Neither now nor for the immediate future is there any way in which we can give the computer that knowledge, despite the fact that such machines have long been the stock-in-trade of fantasy, the Daleks and Marvin the Paranoid Android being the latest creations in a tradition that stretches back to the Golem of sixteenth-century Prague and beyond. However, work in artificial intelligence since the 1960s has shown that computers can be programmed to generate and respond to language appropriately providing that the language relates to knowledge of a restricted world. The classic program in this field was Winograd's SHRDLU which 'knew' about a table-top world of three-dimensional objects. It could manipulate the objects in response to instructions in English, and answer questions about where the objects were, which manipulations were possible and which not, and so forth.

The SHRDLU principle can be applied to a variety of programs allowing the user to practise and explore language. In my TWO STICKS, the computer's 'world of knowledge' is restricted to two 'sticks' labelled A and B that it draws in succession at the top of the

VDU screen. Stick A may be longer than B: or B longer than A: or they may be the same length. The computer randomly decides whether to tell the truth or to lie, and generates a statement accordingly which the player has to identify as true or false. The linguistic complexity of the output depends on the player's current score: at the start of the game it will generate statements such as:

A is longer than B
A and B are the same length
B is not as long as A

while as the game progresses and the player's score mounts, the computer may generate:

A is marginally shorter than B
B is almost as long as A
A and B differ considerably in length
B is half as long again as A.

At the end of twenty turns the player is given a score based on the accuracy and speed of his responses. While TWO STICKS is designed to be played competitively, TIME is more contemplative: the program demonstrates the five ways in which the time may be told in English, the student being simply given the facility to halt the program to study the language at greater leisure, or to delay its appearing on the screen for self-testing. The ability to use the program to observe how the language operates is a feature of John Higgins' remarkable GRAMMARLAND programs which come close to the SHRDLU model in that they not only ask questions about the computer's little 'world of knowledge', but are also able to answer questions about the world.

All the programs referred to above are able to generate language with reference to meaning: that is to say, they know whether a statement is true or false, or (as in GRAMMARLAND) whether it *may* be true. A further dimension to language is that a statement may be appropriate in one context but inappropriate in another. This pragmatic dimension is explored by my LOAN program, which is in the 'exploratory' format already referred to. The computer offers to borrow a sum of money for the user: it asks for information about how much is wanted, and who it is to be borrowed from, and generates a range of appropriate request forms ranging from 'Got 10p on you?' for a close friend to 'I wonder if you could possibly see your way to letting me have an overdraft of £5000?' for a bank manager. In trying out different possibilities the learner can begin to find out how the language changes with situation.

In this paper there has been space only to touch on some of the many ways that the computer may help in learning a foreign language once it is given a generative role in interaction with the learner. There are many more possibilities which have not been covered: for example, the use of computer simulations, and 'conversation generators' such as Weizenbaum's ELIZA. The technology behind the work is new enough, and the ideas unformed enough for this to be an exciting time to be working in the field of computer-assisted language-learning. The best hope for the future is that as many practising teachers as possible should tackle the technology head-on, and try out ideas to discover which work and which do not. In the resulting exchange of ideas it is likely that teachers of foreign languages will find that they have a good deal in common with teachers of a first language, since we are all concerned with effective use of language in communication. This paper is offered as an early and tentative contribution to that exchange.

Software — an historical overview

Dr Jon Coupland, Investigations on Teaching with Microcomputers as an Aid

Over 85 per cent of secondary schools now have at least one microcomputer due to major fund-raising efforts, appeals to parent – teachers associations and local industries, and, in particular, to the Department of Industry half-price funding scheme. The half-price funding scheme has now been extended to primary schools with the declared aim of a micro in every primary school by the end of 1984. Of course, the provision of such computer hardware is only the first hurdle in the search for the most appropriate and effective uses for microcomputers in schools. Immediately the computer arrives in school the next major hurdle is met, namely the acquisition of suitable software, ie, all the sets of instructions (programs) and associated information that have to be fed into the computer. It is also surprising to find that computer software will only work on the particular make of computer on which it was designed. However, with rapid advances in technology this problem may be rectified.

We will approach this overview of software historically. Hopefully this will not only demonstrate the progression of the facilities offered by the software, mirroring the advancing technical capabilities of computers, but also very encouraging signs of software development being driven by the requirements of the practising class teacher.

Probably the first computer programs designed for use in the secondary English curriculum were STORY and HAIKU. In STORY the user is requested to type in a list of words which will then be slotted into a built-in text to provide a complete story. Typically the interaction would occur as follows:

STORY
LET'S MAKE A STORY TOGETHER
FIRST I NEED 11 ADJECTIVES. ADJECTIVES MODIFY A NOUN,
E.G. RED, DIRTY, LARGE.
ADJECTIVE 1? UGLY
ADJECTIVE 2?

The program would then ask for a set of adverbs, nouns, names and locations and then print out the complete story on paper.
Additionally the computer could randomly jumble each set of words and produce a set of stories containing the same words but probably

containing different messages. The program is interesting from many aspects. Probably its most immediate indicator of a future educational value was its capacity for asking for a limited input from the user and producing a long printed output personalized by the user but also accurately typed out. The computer printer does not distinguish between the writing ability of users. It always produces beautifully typed, accurately aligned print; highly motivating for some less able students. Also even this simple program could not be categorized as suitable for either a specific age and ability level or a particular style of classroom management. It could be used to support class discussions, small group work and individual use, with or without a teacher being present, although its use by small groups without a teacher could produce problems with the final request NOW TELL ME A RUDE WORD.

The other early program was HAIKU. This involved the well-known production of 'poetry' by randomly fitting words into a general fixed structure. All the words were usually built into the program and probably its main use was in discussing whether a machine could produce what most people consider to be poetry. A typical product of this program is shown below and it will be clear which words have been randomly slotted into position.

'Now white as the rainbows
Watch gleaming mushrooms in the dunes
And see the rain has crumbled

Now hazy as the fire light
Watch jewelled acorns in the clouds
And bang the snow has cracked

Now hazy as the fire light
Pluck jewelled stars in the waters
And look the tree has dropped

Now brilliant as the dragon
Praise burning poppies in the dunes
And woosh the flame has cracked'

These early programs, although technically very simple, did point the way towards some of the positive aspects of computers in the classroom. In both, the computer is used to jumble information randomly to produce material which is original to both teacher and students. This capability has proved very powerful in a wide range of applications. It means that the computer actually appears to have a personality and one consequence is that the teacher can realistically work alongside the students in joint discussion of the results. These programs also showed the importance of not dismissing a computer implementation of a problem merely because it could be pursued without the computer. The computer was not being used to replace current activities but to complement them, providing a fresh, subtly contrasting environment. It was clear even at these early stages that the only real assessment of the effects of the computer in the curriculum, as with all other innovations, is by direct trials and observation.

With the more general introduction of computers into schools, and in particular the advent of the microcomputer, a popular candidate for computer programmers was HANGMAN. This embodied many of the new facilities offered by the microcomputer — animated graphic displays and the ability to trap the character typed at the keyboard before it is displayed. In HANGMAN, as a key was pressed the program could check if it was a missing character and, if so, display it in the appropriate positions on the screen. There were probably as many teachers and pupils writing hangman programs as we now have writing arcade games. Again HANGMAN produced interesting effects in the classroom and proved capable of use in a wide range of classroom management and teaching styles. It also was an important pointer to future developments as the words stored in the program could very easily be altered. A teacher with very little knowledge of computer programming could modify the possible target words. This capability for teachers essentially to author their own software, even at this simple level, proved very attractive.

It was at this stage of the introduction of computers into schools that large quantities of software were written. The computers were usually acquired by the mathematics department to support the teaching of computer studies, and so naturally the software produced was predominantly biased towards mathematics and science teaching. It is only recently that software has become available to use the computer effectively in other areas of the school curriculum.

Continuing our historical journey we arrive at the creation of ANIMAL. This, initially, was a simple program designed to demonstrate to children the process of classification. Built into the program is a set of questions and then links to other questions or the name of an animal depending on whether we answer yes or no. So a typical progression would be:

DOES IT FLY? NO
IS IT A FISH? NO
IS IT FURRY? YES

The true potential of the program is realized on reaching an animal because instead of telling us the name of the animal it produces another question:

IS IT A GORILLA?

If we reply no, we are asked for the name of the new animal and then, quite logically, a question that will distinguish our new animal from a gorilla. This additional information is then added to that already stored in the computer. This ability to extend the information list immediately moves ANIMAL away from a mere classification program; it becomes a forum for discussion. Since ANIMAL appeared many other similar programs have been developed, perhaps the most sophisticated being SEEK. SEEK makes a virtue of a major limitation of microcomputer display in the classroom, namely the very limited amount of information that can be displayed on a television screen. As shown in the sample screen display below, SEEK only shows a few questions at a time but the user can

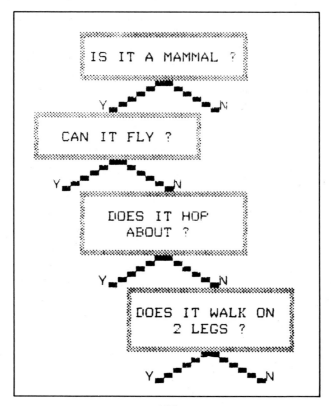

in the creation of his own teaching material suitable to his own style. As will be clear, much of the software discussed here is applicable across the curriculum and will allow us, if we desire it, to break down some of the artificial subject barriers we have at present. It will probably be heartening for teachers of English to note that all the research undertaken into microcomputers in the classroom points to one major effect: namely, that it positively encourages teacher-pupil and pupil-pupil dialogue. The true role of the computer will probably be as a teaching assistant rather than a substitute teacher, supporting the teacher in the creation of an environment with many opportunities for learning and in particular for learning about learning.

Software availability

A listing of STORY and details of HAIKU can be found in *The Best of Creative Computing, Vol 1* by D H Ahl, Creative Computing Press, Moristown, NJ, ISBN 0 916688-01-1. Both programs make no use of graphics and, unusually, the instructions will work on virtually all microcomputers. The availability of the other software discussed is given in detail in the following table for the RML 380Z and BBC microcomputers, where appropriate. Writing a version of HANGMAN should be a straightforward task for most aspiring sixth-form programming students. Versions of ADVENTURE are available for almost all microcomputers and they are widely advertised in the personal computing magazines.

Name	Computer	Supplier
HANGMAN	380Z	AUCBE as below
SEEK	380Z BBC	To be published by Longman
QUERY WORD	380Z 380Z	}AUCBE, Endymion Road, }Hatfield, AL10 8AU
DECODE	380Z	To be published by Longman
ADVENTURE	380Z BBC	Software Production Associates, PO Box 59, Leamington Spa, Warwickshire, CV31 3QA Micro Power Ltd, 8 Regent Street, Chapel Allerton, Leeds, LS7 4PE

Table 1. Availability of software for the RML 380Z and BBC microcomputers

The English teacher and the programmer: how can they talk together?

Jan Bright, Languages Manager, Chelsea College, University of London Computers-in-the-Curriculum Project

English teachers interested in the creative possibilities of the micro may well feel (a) they are the 'poor relations' as far as good educational software is concerned, or (b) thankful that as late starters they can reap the benefit from the experience of those teachers in other subject areas 'who have gone before'. Out of that experience has come an impetus towards innovative and flexible CAL (computer-assisted learning) materials, and away from that rooted in drill and practice or tutorial programs.

The Computers-in-the-Curriculum Project has been working in the field of computer-assisted learning for both the sciences and the humanities since 1973. The maxim of the original Project Director, Bob Lewis, 'to design units that would encourage students to ask "What would happen if..."', has been the starting point for groups of teachers developing CAL material in various subject areas. For example, geography teachers wanted to teach the real implications of the seasonal wind belts, in their influence on climate and weather, etc. A game called WINDS was developed which enables students to simulate navigating a large sailing ship around the oceans. The current position of the ship is indicated on a world map displayed on the TV screen, which also records the line of the ship's voyage from leaving port. This can be used at a variety of levels and for a variety of teaching objectives, eg:

— compass directions
— latitude and longitude
— basic facts about sailing ships
— voyages of discovery.

These simulation and gaming applications of the micro seem to offer more than conventional forms of CAL, involving both motivational and role-playing aspects.

From the perspective of the CIC Project, when teachers are first shown that these kinds of CAL materials already exist within the humanities (and more importantly, given the chance to sit down at a micro and use it!) they are excited and enthusiastic about the potential that is offered to them. They then want to translate their own ideas across on to the micro, and exploit this new resource. This means getting involved in the design and development of CAL programs, and as a direct result it also means becoming aware of some of the realities behind the micro mystique. Although CIC is used to setting up groups, each seems to go through the same learning curve.

The illusion of the micro as a self-determined 'magic box' is soon dispelled. A micro can only do what it is told to do; if what it is told is incorrect, then it will perform its task either incorrectly or not at all! Programming involves the use of a computer language to provide and organize the instructions which control the micro. This requires a blow-by-blow description of what the program is to do. The basic need here is to understand the exactness of specification required. Programming time is nearly always the major component of a unit's development cycle; false expectations about the speed of programming soon disappear.

CIC philosophy and practice is that good educational software is written by teachers for teachers. They do not need to be able to write the program themselves, but they work closely with project programmers throughout the entire design and development process.

Good design should revolve around the educational aims of the program. A clear view of what those aims are forms an essential part of producing good, effective CAL. The programmer will then design and implement the program in terms of those educational aims. For this reason, most project programmers are subject specialists and ex-teachers. The communication of goals and ideas should be made easier for the design team, with contributions coming from any member of the team.

As the development proceeds, ideas about the aims of the program change and progress. The developers will need to clarify their own views as to what usage the pupil or teacher can make of the program in the classroom, and what kind of activities the program will stimulate or encourage. 'What you need to know to describe to the programmer' involves a variety of considerations on both sides, some of which may not be obvious during the initial stages of development, or even during the later stages! They all have an effect on the design and feasibility of the program, and I have sketched in the more important ones below.

Considerations — general and specific
(i) There is a danger of only putting something on a computer because it is there. Existing educational resources may well cope with the problem effectively, the most important resource of all being teachers themselves!

(ii) What age or ability range is the program aimed at?

(iii) Is it intended/designed for individual and/or group work?

(iv) How do you see the program being used by other teachers with different teaching styles? Does the program impose a particular teaching style on the teacher? A good CAL program should adapt to the teacher and not the other way round. Flexibility for both teacher and pupil is an important ingredient of imaginative CAL work.

(v) Does it intrigue or stimulate the children, and does it make them want to come back for more?

(vi) Children are attracted to micros, but although flashing lights, etc, are initially captivating, they can tire with repetition.

(vii) Is the program difficult to use or understand? Does using the program require a teacher to be present?

(viii) How much preparation will the teacher or pupil need to do before they actually use the program?

(ix) What extra written material will need to be developed for use within the program, either as explanation or extensions for the program?

(x) How long does the program take to run? Is it designed for use over a series of lessons?

(xi) Is the program robust and reliable? The pupil must not be able to get lost, nor find that the program has 'fallen over'.

(xii) What kind and size of machine is required to run the program?

(xiii) Can the program be made more transferable? Programs that fully exploit the facilities of a particular micro are likely to be difficult to transfer to another. This limits the number of teachers who can use the program, ie, only those who have access to the same machine as you!

(xiv) What about the programming language the program is to be written in? BASIC (Beginners All-Purpose Symbolic Instruction Code) is the most wide-spread in schools, but it has many different dialects which vary from machine to machine. Writing a program in a particular dialect may again make the program less transferable.

(xv) Also, as its name suggests, BASIC is hardly a sophisticated language. A lot of ingenuity may be required of the programmer to achieve the educational aims of the program because of the combined restrictions of languages and machines. Possible areas of difficulty for the programmer will need to be discussed with the team so that alternatives can be thought of. For example, can we modify the screen layout/presentation? This 'thrashing-out' process often invokes surprise that a seemingly small change in specification may lead to a disproportionate number of reprogramming headaches. It may be necessary to modify some of the original ideas without losing the educational value, in order to make the program more transferable, and so more accessible to teachers.

Just considering these factors may seem a daunting task, particularly for teachers who are new to the development of CAL. The enthusiasm generated by their first impression may well be followed by a suspicion that here is yet another piece of technology that doesn't live up to expectations. To which I can only say 'Stay with it — the results may surprise you'.

Developing good CAL is not easy, and the development process can be long and demanding. Each unit we produce goes through initial and subsequent programming, trials, altered design and rewriting, and so on up to publication. As one of our teachers said: 'Producing a CAL unit is rather like Monopoly, just when I think I'm going to pass GO, the chance card sends me back for another rewrite'.

The more imaginative and creative uses of CAL can be frustrating but also fascinating to produce. There is a wealth of software available which may appear to be very glamorous indeed, but it does not necessarily achieve its educational aims. From our own experience, 'The provision of software within a pack that enhances direct student interaction as opposed to passive reception is not only an asset, but one which reflects clearly to the teacher the Project's rationale for CAL'. The sense of achievement in producing good, flexible, innovative material more than compensates for any frustrations along the way.

References

LEWIS, R and WANT, D, 'Educational computing at Chelsea, 1969-1979', Proceedings of IFIP TC3 Working Conference, 1979, in Lewis, R and Tagg, D (eds), *Computer-Assisted Learning: scope, progress and limits,* North Holland Publishing Co, 1980; Heinemann (paperback), 1981

WATSON, DERYN, 'Computer-assisted learning in the humanities', Proceedings of IFIP World Conference 1981, Lausanne, in Lewis, R and Tagg, D (eds), *Computers in Education,* North Holland Publishing Co, 1981

Further reading

ADAMS, ANTHONY and JONES, ESMOR, *Teaching Humanities in the Microelectronics Age,* Open University Press, 1983

AHL, DAVID, 'Computers in language arts', in Lecame, O and Lewis, R (eds), *Computers and Education,* IFIP, pp 889-94, North Holland Publishing Co, 1975

CHANDLER, DANIEL, 'The potential of the microcomputer in the English classroom', in Adams, A (ed), *New Directions in English Teaching,* Falmer Press, 1982

CHANDLER, DANIEL, 'Are we still living in Lagado?, text of a lecture on microelectronics and the humanities delivered at the University of Cambridge, Microelectronics Education Programme, 1981

CHANDLER, DANIEL, 'The games some pupils play', *Educational Computing,* **2**, 10, p 28, November 1981

CHANDLER, DANIEL, 'Great expectations', *Educational Computing,* **3**, 9, pp 24-25, November 1982

COLLINS, ALLAN, BRUCE, BERTRAM C and RUBIN, ANDEE, 'Microcomputer-based writing activities for the upper elementary grades' in Proceedings of the Fourth International Congress of the Society for Applied Learning Technology, 1982

HARRISON, COLIN, 'The textbook as an endangered species: the implications of economic decline and technological advance on the place of reading in learning, *Oxford Review of Education,* **7**, 3, pp 231-240, 1981

HIGGINS, JOHN (ed), *Computers and English Language Teaching,* British Council, 1982

LONGWORTH, NORMAN, 'We're moving into the information society. What shall we teach the children?', Computer Education, pp 17-19, June 1981

PAPERT, SEYMOUR, *Mindstorms: children, computers and powerful ideas,* Harvester Press, 1980

SHARPLES, MIKE, *Poetry from LOGO*, Working Paper No 30, Department of Artificial Intelligence, University of Edinburgh, June 1978

SHARPLES, MIKE, and ROSS, P M (eds), 'Microcomputers and creative writing' in Howe, J A M *Microcomputers in Secondary Education: issues and techniques,* Kogan Page, 1981

SHARPLES, MIKE 'A computer-based teaching scheme for creative writing', in Lewis, R and Tagg, D (eds) *Computers in Education,* North Holland Publishing Co, 1981

Useful addresses

Advisory Unit for Computer-Based Education (AUCBE)
    Endymion Road, Hatfield, Herts AL10 8AU

Computers in Education as a Resource (CEDAR)
    Imperial College Computer Centre, Exhibition Road,
    London SW7 2BX

Computers-in-the-Curriculum Project (CIC)
    Chelsea College, Hudson Buildings, 552 Kings Road,
    London SW10 0UA

Investigations in Teaching with Microcomputers as an Aid (ITMA)
    College of St Mark and St John, Derriford Road, Plymouth PL6 8BH

Microelectronics Education Programme (MEP)
    Cheviot House, Newcastle-upon-Tyne Polytechnic, Coach Lane
    Campus, Newcastle-upon-Tyne NE7 7XA

National Association for the Teaching of English (NATE)
    49 Broomgrove Road, Sheffield S10 2NA

Index